Frederick J Lombardo
3233 Adams Ct
Fairfax VA 22030

Developing the World Class Information Systems Organization

Volume 3

Books and Training Products From QED

DATABASE

Data Analysis: The Key to Data Base Design
The Data Dictionary: Concepts and Uses
DB2: The Complete Guide to Implementation and Use
Logical Data Base Design
DB2 Design Review Guidelines
DB2: Maximizing Performance of Online Production Systems
Entity-Relationship Approach to Logical Data Base Design
How to Use ORACLE SQL*PLUS
ORACLE: Building High Performance Online Systems
Embedded SQL for DB2: Application Design and Programming
SQL for dBASE IV
Introduction to Data and Activity Analysis
ORACLE Design Review Guidelines
Using DB2 to Build Decision Support Systems
How to Use SQL for DB2

SYSTEMS ENGINEERING

Handbook of Screen Format Design
Managing Projects: Selecting and Using PC-Based Project Management Systems
The Complete Guide to Software Testing
A User's Guide for Defining Software Requirements
A Structured Approach to Systems Testing
Practical Applications of Expert Systems
Expert Systems Development: Building PC-Based Applications
Storyboard Prototyping: A New Approach to User Requirements Analysis
The Software Factory: Managing Software Development and Maintenance
Data Architecture: The Information Paradigm
Advanced Topics in Information Engineering

MANAGEMENT

CASE: The Potential and the Pitfalls
Strategic and Operational Planning for Information Services
The State of the Art in Decision Support Systems
The Management Handbook for Information Center and End-User Computing
Disaster Recovery: Contingency Planning and Program Analysis

MANAGEMENT (cont'd)

Winning the Change Game
Information Systems Planning for Competitive Advantage
Critical Issues in Information Processing Management and Technology
Developing the World Class Information Systems Organization
The Technical Instructor's Handbook: From Techie to Teacher
Collision: Theory vs. Reality in Expert System
How to Automate Your Computer Center: Achieving Unattended Operations
Ethical Conflicts in Information and Computer Science, Technology, and Business

DATA COMMUNICATIONS

Data Communications: Concepts and Solutions
Designing and Implementing Ethernet Networks
Network Concepts and Architectures
Open Systems: The Guide to OSI and its Implementation
VAX/VMS: Mastering DCL Commands and Utilities

PROGRAMMING

VSAM Techniques: Systems Concepts and Programming Procedures
How to Use CICS to Create On-Line Applications: Methods and Solutions
DOS/VSE/SP Guide for Systems Programming: Concepts, Programs, Macros, Subroutines
Systems Programmer's Problem Solver
VSAM: Guide to Optimization and Design
MVS/TSO: Mastering CLISTS
MVS/TSO: Mastering Native Mode and ISPF
VAX/VMS: Mastering DCL Commands and Utilities

SELF-PACED TRAINING

SQL as a Second Language
Building Online Production Systems with DB2 (Video)
Introduction to UNIX (CBT)
Building Production Applications with ORACLE (Video)

For Additional Information or a Free Catalog contact

QED INFORMATION SCIENCES, INC. • P. O. Box 82-181 • Wellesley, MA 02181
Telephone: 800-343-4848 or 617-237-5656

Developing the World Class Information Systems Organization

Volume 3

The Dooley Group

QED Information Sciences, Inc.
Wellesley, Massachusetts

© 1990 by QED Information Sciences, Inc.
P.O. Box 82-181
Wellesley, MA 02181

All rights reserved. No part of the material protected by this copyright notice may be reproduced or utilized in any form or by any means, electronic or mechanical, including photocopying, recording, or by any information storage and retrieval systems, without written permission from the copyright owner.

International Standard Book Number: 0-89435-371-3
International Standard Serial Number: 1046-7238

Printed in the United States of America
90 91 92 10 9 8 7 6 5 4 3 2 1

Contents

vii *From the Publisher*

1 *Where Should the Information Systems Function Go In the 1990s?*
Ferdinand J. Setaro

15 *The New Computer Economics*
Jerome Kanter

21 *The Information Spiral: Toward a New Paradigm for Information Management*
Louann K. Reilly

31 *Information Systems: Messages from the Past, Lessons for the Future*
Jerome Kanter

39 *An Emerging Methodology for Managing Large Systems Projects*
Robert C. Ford, Peter M. Ginter, Andrew C. Rucks, James B. Dilworth, J.W. Mitchell

49 *The Art of Managing Upward*
Richard E. Dooley

57 *Everybody Wins: The Theory W Project Manager*
Robert Lambert

65 *Introducing New Technology Through Change Management: A Human Factors Approach*
Christopher Bond and Vincent J. DeFazio

73 *The Basics of Total Quality Management*
Thomas H. Berry and Ferdinand J. Setaro

77 *Total Quality Management in an Information Systems Environment*
Thomas H. Berry and Ferdinand J. Setaro

87 *Just What Good Is an Information Systems Architecture Anyway?*
John M. Blair and Ralph D. Loftin

105 *We Just Don't Respect Requirements*
Steven J. Andriole

123 *Implementing an Information Engineering Environment at National Liberty Corporation*
Peter Cola

129 *It's Time for MIS to Change the Image of Fax*
Ralph D. Loftin

From the Publisher

In December of 1986, I was invited by Dick Dooley and Ralph Loftin to attend the Dooley Group's "Fifth Annual Executives' Conference" in Phoenix. The focus of the conference was on the effective and efficient harnessing of technology, computers, systems, information, and people to an organization"s business objectives. The presenters were excellent and the participation and open dialogue of the senior executive attendees added a dimension seldom found in such a meeting.

The focus was on practical issues with emphasis on how to achieve success today while preparing for the eventualities of tomorrow. There was serious dialogue about today's issues, not the usual conference hyperbole and superficial presentations. There was a give-and-take that forced serious thinking about what information processing is today, where are we headed, and how will we get there.

Of particular interest to me was the Dooley Group"s "Gestalt" idea. Seldom do attendees share a common view. This group was no exception. The Dooley Group presenters focused on the varied views and the need to be aware of them while managing the information resource. It was obvious that each attendee went away from the meeting with a collection of ideas for solving the problems of managing information processing.

I asked myself how we could bring this valuable information to a wider audience. I spoke with members of the Dooley Group: Dick, Ralph, John Blair, Ferdie Setaro, Ted Reid, Tom Cavanaugh, and others. We all agreed it was a difficult task. The missing ingredient in written material is the open dialogue, the "question-asker," the issue-raiser," and the motivator to encourage managers to take time out of busy schedules to read. Could we provide this? Yes, but only if you, the managers, are willing to use the material as the basis of your own "focus" sessions.

You can do this by sharing the material with your senior IS management staff. Every 2 to 4 weeks a reading from the material should be assigned to your senior management team. You, or one of your staff, will be the moderator who encourages discussion, re-thinking, and accepting of other approaches. The moderator will have the following responsibilities:

1. Prepare the format of the meeting.
2. Set the meeting agenda.
3. Begin the meeting and control the direction.
4. Encourage participation, new ideas, open-mindedness, and innovative thinking.
5. Provide transition to new ideas, thoughts, and topics.
6. Summarize points along the way.
7. Conclude the meeting with a summary and an action plan.

The idea is to brainstorm around the theme of the reading, focus on your problems, and not be afraid to expand the thinking. Be sure you encourage new ideas and approaches. By doing this, you will cross-fertilize ideas with your management team and take advantage of different perspectives.

These "forums" should be short 1-to-2 hour sessions that encourage open-minded discussion among all the participants. It seems to me that these sessions help build team skills and teach collaboration and the dynamics of group work. This may be by far the greatest benefit your organization will accrue. This is what leadership is all about.

Those of you who know the Dooley Group are aware that it is a select federation of "seniors," all experienced in corporate/business processes, who provide a broad counseling service in the successful planning, implementation, and utilization of information systems and computer technology. We look forward to continually publishing new work created by this talented group.

As a publisher, I am excited to be able to publish the Dooley Group's work. As an executive, I have already benefited from the readings.

Edwin F. Kerr
Publisher
QED Information Sciences, Inc.

WHERE SHOULD THE INFORMATION SYSTEMS FUNCTION GO IN THE 1990s?

Ferdinand J. Setaro

In the late 1980s, companies began to reorganize the IS function to fit the new paradigm of IS and the business function. That process will continue and grow in the '90s.

The author of this article once consulted to an IS company which had been reorganized so often the employees began to refer to their "organization chart du jour."

The author's experience in doing organization design consulting revealed that most reorganizations — and not just IS reorganization — are done by managers who have never studied the various organizational designs, and the pros and cons of each.

This article describes and illustrates the major organizational design options available and some of the reasons for choosing any particular one. The author includes the organization model he believes best suits most IS shops he has seen; the one he has named the "distributed organization."

INTRODUCTION

Where should the Information Systems function go in the 1990s? Not "away." Only someone totally frustrated by IS technology or IS people would say that today.

However, organizationally speaking, the Information Systems function should no longer be looked at in the binary manner we tended to use in the '70s and the '80s.

In the '70s we almost all centralized the function and built tremendous centralized "big-iron" shops. Then with the advent of the PC and "tiny iron," we spent most of the '80s trying to dismantle the centralized information function and give it all to the users — who were stealing it anyway.

For the '90s, let me suggest that we think about being contextual, not binary. Thinking contextually leads me to say, as Yogi might if he were an organization design consultant, "The best organization for your organization is the best organization for your organization." Or, as Harvey Sherman, who *was* an organization design consultant, put it, "It all depends."*

---
*It All Depends *by Harvey Sherman, University of Alabama Press, 1966. One of the best, most practical books ever written on organization design.*

What's the right organization for your Information Systems function? It all depends on the context of your organization. Since I don't know your context, I can't make a recommendation.

What I can do is help you think the question through. I'll describe the basic organizational structures and let you put them into your context.

There is also a new structure emerging — in the real world or perhaps only in my head. I haven't quite figured it out yet. You may find it interesting to think about. It's included at the very end of the article.

I will also cheat a bit. I do have a preferred organization design which fits most enterprises. It is the "distributed organizational structure." But that's only my opinion. I hope this article will help you form your own.

When talking about *how* to organize an enterprise, one can describe a multitude of themes, variations on the themes, and combinations of those themes and variations.

However, when one looks at *why* an enterprise is organized, the myriad combinations can be limited. Furthermore, when there is a specific question involved, in this case around the placement of the Information Systems function, then we can narrow it down even further.

For our purposes, we need cover only six basic organizational themes and one variation. There is a seventh theme emerging, but that requires further study, so it will be treated only briefly at the end of the article.

My basic definition of organizing is "structuring organizational resources to accomplish an objective in a given context." Here are some thoughts on each part of that definition, starting with the word "objective."

An enterprise's objective tends to be stable for a substantial period of time. This means we can organize, i.e., "structure organizational resources," for that stable period. However, we must reexamine our specific organization every time our objective changes.

Just as the enterprise's objectives can change, so can the "given context" in which that enterprise exists. When the enterprise's context changes, many things must be reexamined, including the way the enterprise is organized. Such examination may reveal that the enterprise should change its organization.

This article focuses on that part of the definition concerning the structuring of organizational resources. The "resources" are primarily authority, functions, and lines of communication, including coordination and time. We are going to look at the six basic organization themes or, as we will call them from now on, six basic organizational structures.

The structures are most easily described if considered in sets. Each set consists of two contrasting, though not necessarily opposing, structures. I call the three organization structure sets:

- functional—product
- centralized—decentralized
- matrix—distributed

In any enterprise, several of the six may be combined. Also, at different levels in an enterprise, there may be different organizational structures.

We will *not* cover a distinction often found in organizational design treatises — the difference between line and staff. That's because, organizationally, I don't believe it is a valid distinction, except in specialized circumstances.

One other element is missing. People. The proper way to think through an exercise in organizing is to consider the functions first. Construct the organization. Then find the people who fit the structure *or* change the planned structure to fit the existing people. In real life, we generally do some of both. As you will see, to give some examples, this article has to refer to people.

One final note. For simplicity's sake, the different structures are illustrated by using a company that manufactures three kinds of products — passenger cars, light trucks, and military tanks. We also cover only five of the many functions found in an organization: the function of the Chief Executive Office (CEO); Marketing; Production; Finance; and Information Systems. We will be moving the Information Systems function to show the differences in organizations.

All the functions in our organization will be shown in rectangles except for the Information Systems function, which will be shown in a circle or semicircle to make the changes easier to follow.

FUNCTIONAL ORGANIZATION/PRODUCT ORGANIZATION

An enterprise is first organized in one of these two primary ways. The differences are where and how work gets done. For simplicity, no Information Systems function is shown in these first two illustrations. This company makes passenger cars, light trucks, and tanks. The functions shown are Production, Marketing, and Finance.

In the functional organization, activities are grouped on the basis of specialized skills. Each function is supervised separately. Accountability is compartmentalized. (Figure 1)

In the product organization, the activities necessary to produce, market, and finance a given product or a given service *and* the commensurate accountabilities are grouped together under a single manager. (Figure 2) This is sometimes called a project organization structure, especially in high-tech companies.

There are major benefits of the functional organization:

- Initially it is more cost-effective.
- It develops technical expertise rapidly.
- It fosters application of that expertise to The work situation.

Figure 1. Functional organization.

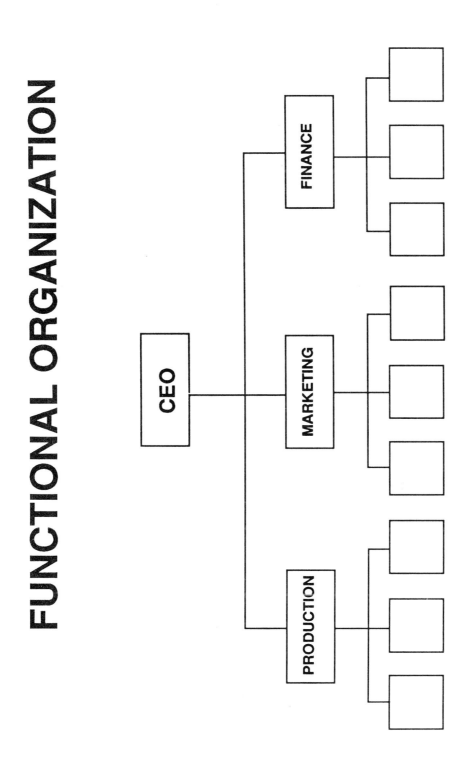

Figure 2. Product organization.

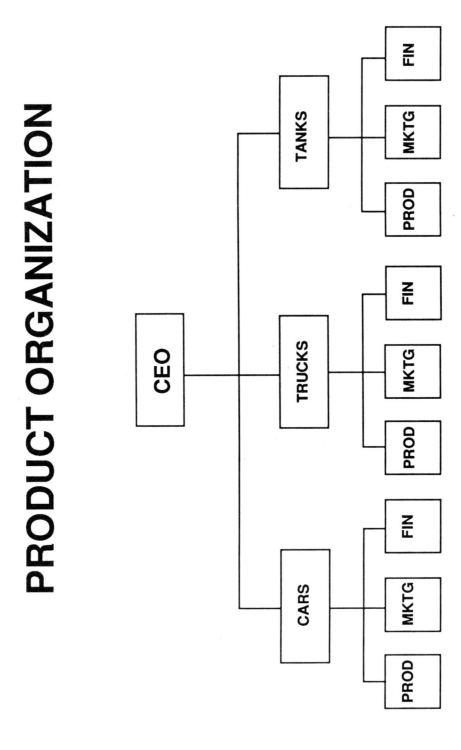

Major benefits of the product organization include:

- It fixes profit responsibility more easily.
- Coordination is easier.
- Lower-level employees are closer to the end product.
- It focuses more on the purpose of the enterprise.

It should be noted that in the paired structures what is identified as a benefit for one structure *tends* to be a penalty in the other. This is true for functional/product and will be true for the other structures.

CENTRALIZED ORGANIZATION/ DECENTRALIZED ORGANIZATION

This category has to do primarily with decision making and resource distribution.

In the centralized organization (Figure 3), decision making and resources are kept in one area, as illustrated by the Information Systems circle. Information Systems becomes an additional functional area to marketing, finance, and production.

In the decentralized structure (Figure 4), decision making and resources are given to each functional area, as shown by the Information Systems semicircles attached to each function.

Major benefits of centralizing a function include:

- decreased cost
- initially, higher-quality decisions
- consistent policies and their application
- ease of dealing with large technological shifts

Major benefits of decentralizing a function include:

- faster decisions
- more original ideas/involvement from more employees
- greater involvement with the corporation's business

- easier application of technology to each function

CAPTURED FUNCTION ORGANIZATION

There is a variation on the centralized/decentralized theme called the Captured Function. (Figure 5)

Look at the placement of Information Systems. It is centralized but placed under another function. The Finance function will get its needs fulfilled. However, *only* if there is time left over do the other functions get their needs fulfilled.

The captured function structure was fine for Information Systems when the first electronic data processors were taking the place of the old electric accounting machines (punched card equipment). However, as computers got to be more sophisticated, the captured function organization often prevented Information Systems from making its potential contribution to the company bottom line. The main advantages of the captured organization structure are realized when the captured function (Information Systems) is expected to serve the master function (Finance) almost exclusively.

MATRIX ORGANIZATION/DISTRIBUTED ORGANIZATION

To a certain extent, these two types are hybrids of the first four. They have been developed primarily to accommodate the impact on organizations of information, information technology, and product management techniques.

The Matrix structure (Figure 6) provides a way to combine functional and decentralized structures. It puts information systems resources in both the functional area and in the mainframe centralized Information Systems function.

The innovative but also most difficult aspect of this type of organization is that it breaks the organizational principle of "unity of command." This principle says that no function should report to two higher functions for the same responsibility.

Figure 3. Centralized organization.

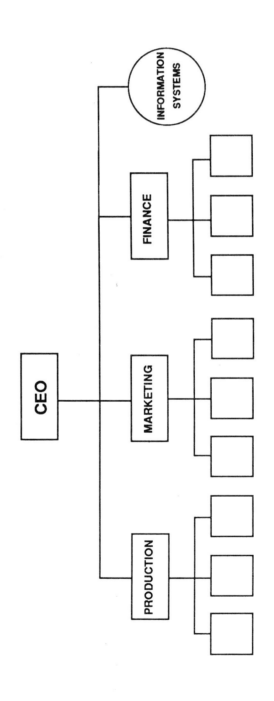

Figure 4. Decentralized organization.

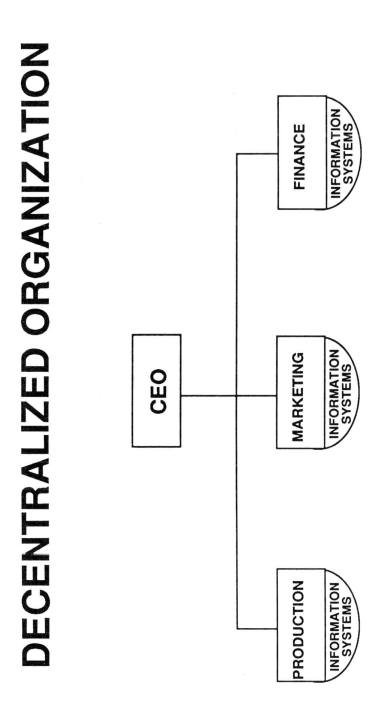

Figure 5. Captured function organization.

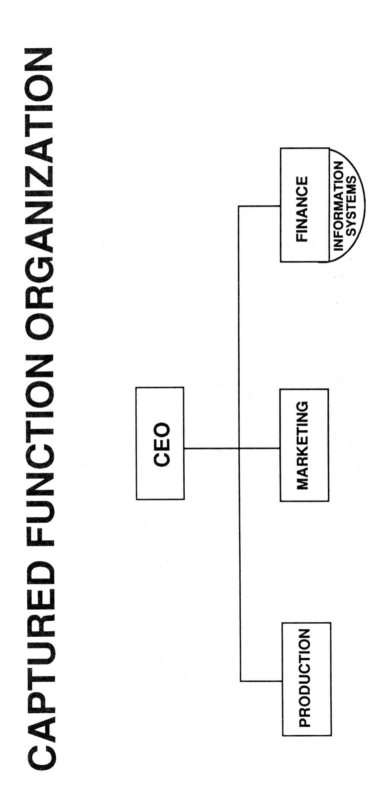

Figure 6. Distributed organization.

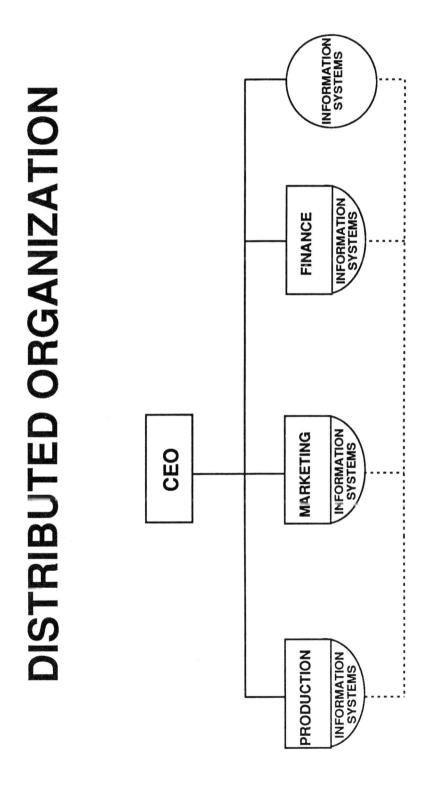

For example, if a person reports to two different people, then success requires that both bosses (for instance, the VP Finance and the head of the centralized Information Systems function) must recognize that they have to collaborate and reach consensus before they actually talk or give orders to the matrixed subordinate.

The chart for the distributed organization (Figure 7), looks the same as the Matrix chart except that the lines drawn from the decentralized information system units to the IS function are dotted, indicating that the distributed resources report to one function but are also strongly related to another. To make distributed structures succeed, all involved must have an acute awareness of lateral relationships. The ability to work lateral relationships is an absolute *sine qua non* for the distributed organization to succeed. The five lateral relations are:

1. **WORKFLOW:** This type of relationship includes interaction with any manager who is in charge of production steps that precede or follow the steps that occur in your own department.

2. **SERVICE:** Interaction with a manager who provides common services for many managers is a service relationship.

3. **ADVISORY:** An advisory relationship is one in which you seek the advice of another manager or one in which another manager seeks advice from you.

4. **MONITORING:** In this category is your relationship with an individual or group having the authority to assess, evaluate, or "give a grade" to your results.

5. **STABILIZATION:** Stabilization managers are those whose approval you must gain before initiating some action — thus ensuring that managerial decisions are in harmony with overall organization policy and objectives.

Of course, any particular manager is not relegated to playing just one role. In fact, most staff departments play several roles. Probably the most obvious example of this is the Human Resources department. When Human Resources does the first screening of prospective employees, it's wearing its service hat. When it suggests to the supervisor an appropriate disciplinary penalty, that's advising. When it surveys departmental absenteeism, Human Resources is functioning as a monitor. And when it turns down a pay recommendation as out of line with company policy, that's stabilization.

In the distributed structure, the Corporate IS function would usually relate to the departmental IS functions in all relationships.

Assuming you want teamwork, one of the major advantages of the distributed organization structure is that it almost forces people to work as a team. Another is that it helps assure that the functional department managements do not delegate away the responsibility for information.

RECOMMENDATION

Given the current state of technology, I believe that the distributed organization structure is best for most organizations. After all, it only recognizes the reality that there are many more decentralized MIPs in the departments than there are in the big-iron shop — even where the formal organization structure is centralized!

Most of the big-iron bigots among us who said personal computing and micros would go the way of the hula hoop were trampled to death in the early '80s by the rush of users after their own computing power.

The distribution of computing power plus project orientation gave rise to the distributed organization structure. All I'm saying is that it's still not too late to get in front of the mob and become its leader. If you don't have a distributed organization, please consider it.

Figure 7. Distributed organization.

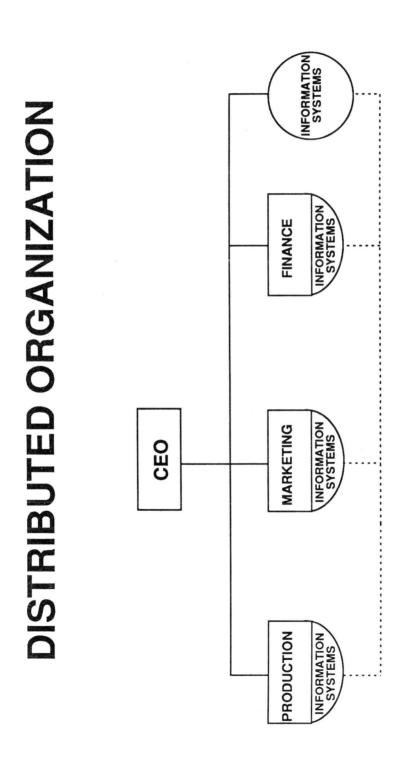

Figure 8. The virtual organization.

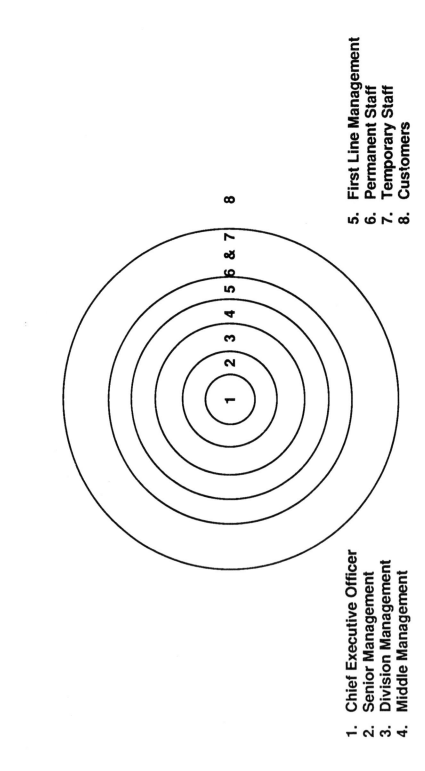

EPILOGUE

Last but not least is the emerging organizational form I call the virtual organization. It is my version of what some are calling the "wheel" or "network" organization. I have been working on it on and off for the past year or so. However, I still can't describe it in a few words. Figure 8 is release 1.5 of my design, with more to come. I believe it will be a three-dimensional model. I am not yet satisfied with the theory nor the illustration. Nevertheless, it is food for thought.

I call this structure "virtual" because it can be designed to work like most of the preceding organizational structures. If there is any possible application to information systems specifically, we'll have to talk it through. Write me c/o QED.

ABOUT THE AUTHOR

Ferdie Setaro is the Managing Director of TLE Consultants, a member of The Dooley Group. He also holds the position of Organization Development and Training Officer for The Vanguard Group of Investment Companies, one of the nation's fastest growing financial services organizations, and the leading no-load mutual fund company.

His IS consulting focuses on linking IS to the business and improving its organization, people, and total quality management. He has managed and taught, consulted and written about the non-technical aspects of DP and IS for over 25 years. His early works include "How to Use the Computer as a Management Tool," AMACOM, 1972, and "Auditing MIS," 1974.

He has more recently been published by the Center for Information Management Studies, the Association of Internal Management Consultants, and QED Information Sciences.

THE NEW COMPUTER ECONOMICS

Jerome Kanter

Computer projects are often evaluated in terms of the number of people displaced (aka "fired").

Of course, the early estimates of "saved" headcount were never achieved, at least not in a way that was satisfactory to the accountants. Jokes about how many times that a position was "saved" by computer projects usually accompanied most estimates.

We are finally realizing that positions "saved" is not the real measure of computer projects. The real measure is now more likely in terms of "new markets served," "new products delivered," or improved customer retention.

Positive thinking is new thinking when it comes to computer economics.

When I was a systems analyst, we justified computer applications by the tangible benefits they produced. In the case of an inventory system, it reduced the number of administrative people and also decreased the average level of inventory to support a given service level. That was nice and neat. But now things have changed and the systems we work on do not necessarily reduce costs; they increase revenue and provide strategic benefits. The systems are aimed at giving a company a competitive edge. Information becomes a valued resource that can provide senior management with powerful decision-making tools.

The examples are legion: the ones most widely used are McKesson Corporation, American Hospital Supply, and American Airlines.[1] Each of these companies used information as a strategic resource to enhance and differentiate its products and services from competition. Ben Heineman, then President and CEO of Northwest Industries, used a computer terminal an average of three hours a day, literally to manage his company, often writing his own programs, accessing internal and external data and analyzing the impact of alternate strategies.[2]

The executives who have realized the near-term benefits and long-term opportunities of strategic information systems understand that traditional accounting methods and cost displacement models cannot be used to fully justify these innovative uses of information systems. They concede that the benefits, though vital to reaching business objectives, are mostly intangible. They are convinced, however, that although the returns from these systems are not always measurable, they can be vital to a company's future success.

However, I see a backlash from senior managers who have not yet seen information systems used in a strategic way within their own companies. They have become a bit skeptical of the grandiose results that have been claimed, and are looking for more tangible proof that they should invest in these systems. Likewise a review of the current literature on the subject does not reveal "hard" benefits, based on a pre- and post-return on investment analysis.

Though cost displacement and cost avoidance are not the only, and maybe not the major, determinants of value, the fundamental concept of quantifying project benefits and performing a return on investment analysis is still important in evaluating strategic information systems. Furthermore, if an assessment is not made at the outset, there is no base point by which to measure actual results. This is why we hear broad sweeping statements of successes of strategic information systems with scant, if any, mention of specifics. Strategic systems have been talked about for some time now — they may have gone from "concept to cliche while bypassing meaning."[3] Tangible benefits can provide that "meaning."

THREE GENERIC COMPETITIVE STRATEGIES

A popular construct these days is that of the "value chain." As described by Porter & Millar,[4] the construct breaks down the things a company does to conduct its business into functions called "value activities." The "value activities" start with inbound logistics through operations, outbound logistics, and finish with sales and service. The price that customers are willing to pay for a product or service represents the "value" that the company creates. To the extent that the "value" is greater than the cost to produce the product or service, the company is profitable. The "value chain" helps develop "leverage points" where cost can be contained or customer "value" can be developed. A company gains competitive advantage over its competitors by either (1) performing these "value activities" at lower cost, (2) differentiating its product or service by the "value activities," or (3) filling the needs of a specialized market by the "value activities."

The latter are termed the three generic strategies that give a customer a competitive edge. Porter and Millar argue that each "value" activity can be influenced by information technology, increasingly so with the expanding hardware and software capabilities and the continued dramatic reduction in the cost of information technology, particularly in the hardware area. However, though their analysis gives excellent qualitative or intangible benefits from information technology, they do not present any help in developing a process to quantify the "value." In all fairness, this is not the intent of their writing, but very few others have attempted it either. Let's now turn to possible approaches to quantify the benefits of using information technology within each of the three generic competitive strategy areas.

THE LOW-COST STRATEGY

If a company follows the low-cost producer strategy, applications that take cost out of the product or service are considered strategic information systems. Tangible benefits are relatively easy to find in this situation. An example is automating a manual input process so that what is being done by 15 clerks will be accomplished by 5. Another tangible example is an inventory control system which reduces average inventory carried by $1,000,000. The carrying costs of that inventory, let's say 20%, create an annual saving of $200,000.

The aim of General Motor's new Saturn plant in Tennessee is to produce a new small automobile line to compete with foreign cars. Manufacturing savings from computer-aided design and computer-aided manufacturing systems are projected by comparing new production processes with existing GM fabrication and assembly plants. The objective is to gain market share by being able to offer the lowest price.

There are several companies that are marketing IBM personal computer clones. These are personal computers that duplicate the logic and circuitry of the IBM personal computer line. They differ from the IBM compatibles, which, while able to run the software that runs on the IBM machines, are not identical in hardware structure. They are hardware rather than software compatible. Therefore, many IBM compatibles have functionality that goes beyond the IBM model; however, the clones do only what their IBM equivalent can do.

As one might imagine, the clones rely solely on a low-cost strategy — that's their only competitive edge. Therefore, they must assemble the cheapest combination of components they can provide: memory chips, boards, power supplies, disk controllers, disks, printer boards, printers, keyboards, etc. An information system that can abet this low-cost strategy is vital to success, like a database of component items with associated costs and supplies so that when there is a change in costs, they can immediately shift vendors or combinations of components. A simulation model can project the best combination of parts and components to produce the lowest cost and historically show what cost savings can be attributed to the information model.

DIFFERENTIATED PRODUCT OR SERVICE STRATEGY

Information systems that support the other two generic strategies are more difficult to justify.

However, I differ from traditional thinkers in that I believe many of the benefits emanating from information systems that support these strategies can be assessed and made tangible. For example, putting terminals in key customer offices supports a differentiated product service, as it makes it easier for customers to buy from that supplier than its competitor. In so doing, it locks in the customer and also increases sales. This is the strategy that was employed by American Hospital Supply. I would ask the question: How much more will our customers buy from us? Estimates of increased revenues can be determined by survey methods, extrapolation techniques, or the assessment of results of similar systems. If a key customer purchased $800,000 from us in a year at a 22% profit margin, a 10% sales increase might be projected due to the new ordering system. This translates into a tangible profit margin benefit of $17,600.

Another question I would ask is how many customers are normally lost in a year and how many fewer will be lost with the new system? If the answer is ten currently and the new system reduces that to eight, the tangible benefit would be $44,000 (2 × average profit margin per customer of $22,000). There are assumptions here, but assumptions are also made in projecting tangible benefits.

Another technique is a break-even analysis. Coleco differentiated its Cabbage Patch doll by giving each doll a name and providing adoption papers to each new owner upon completion of an adoption form. Thereafter, Coleco sends a birthday card on the anniversary of the purchase of the doll. Obviously an information system is required to keep a database on the millions of dolls that are sold each year and their owners. Again, these figures are conjecture only, but suppose the profit margin on each doll is $5. It is feasible that before launching such a program, a pilot market survey or a review with retail marketing consultants could pinpoint the contribution of this feature to sales. If the computer system to handle the paperwork requires an investment of $250,000 and an annual operating cost of $500,000, it becomes clear that 150,000 dolls would have to be sold to cover the investment and a year's operating cost. This brings a clearer perspective in deciding whether the Cabbage Patch registration system is a desirable project.

SPECIALIZED MARKET STRATEGY

The Chrysler Corporation has a specific market niche with its Jeep line, selling to what might be called the luxury summer home population or camping market. This four-wheel drive market is vital to Chrysler (and was the chief reason it purchased the failing American Motors Corporation several years ago), and an information system that abets this strategy is in the competitive edge category. Letters are sent to Jeep Wagoneer owners, offering them a VIP identification card and special service plans emphasizing that the owner has acquired a special car and will be treated accordingly. The VIP support system seeks to establish brand loyalty and also to encourage Jeep owners to act as references to prospective buyers. A computer system that facilitates this process is an important asset to Chrysler.

Suppose, in the case of Wagoneers, customer loyalty traditionally has been 60% (these figures are conjecture only). If the special service program for Wagoneer owners increases that percentage 5% and if 50,000 Wagoneers are sold each year, this will result in 2,500 additional sales. The profit on the 2,500 automobiles can then be compared to the investment and costs to develop and maintain this VIP customer service.

Fidelity Investments, like many investment and banking institutions, is going after an emerging market segment, the home computer market. Fidelity has extended a service to the home wherein a customer can gain access to investment information (broad economic trends and statistics, as well as individual company product and financial data). In addition, the home investor has access to real-time stock quotes and can place buy and sell orders via his home computer tied to Dow-Jones information services and Fidelity computer systems. This is a good example of focus on a special market segment, and indeed Fidelity, according to industry statistics, has captured about half of the on-line brokerage business originating from the home. Though this is still a relatively new and untried market, it is possible to project the economic benefits from relative levels of market penetration. Indeed, Fidelity did just that. They calculated the growth of the home computer market and the percentage of that market interested in home investing. Then from an analysis of their competitors, they projected a market share. Usage, brokerage, and management fees were compared to the costs of setting up the network on a pro forma basis. There are intangible benefits as well, as this application is a model for other extensions into the home computer market. However, it is possible to derive a reasonable return on investment analysis based on the tangibles.

On the investment side, there is a clearer picture of the elements to be considered. These elements include hardware and software investment, outside services, people costs, supplies and materials, telecommunications, overhead, and other cost elements associated with the IS budget. Not to be overlooked are the costs associated with end users such as training, education, and the additional but temporary start-up support expense. For blockbuster projects, costs should be projected on a multiyear basis, as they may differ dramatically from the first year to the second and third. Sometimes it is difficult to be exact, but this should not prevent the sizing of projects in order to rank them as to benefits versus cost (Return on Investment).

BENEFIT/COST AWARENESS

One additional but crucial element is to obtain senior management "ownership" of the particular strategic systems approach. A high-level executive who has the vision of what the system can do for the company should be prepared to stand behind the assumptions and the benefits projected for the system. In the case of strategies that reduce costs, this will likely be the Vice President of Engineering or Manufacturing. In the case of strategies that differentiate the product or fill the needs of a specialized market, this will most likely be the Vice President of Sales and Marketing.

It is an interesting phenomenon that Information System people are usually much more aware of costs than the ultimate user or benefactor of the system. IS people deal with the technology and know the investment necessary to provide the hardware, software, and people cost necessary to implement an application. On the other hand, the users are normally much more aware of the benefits of the system. They are better able to measure both tangible and intangible benefits. This leads to the following simple construct with the basic but important message: an awareness of both IS and users is necessary to build a business case for any proposed new system.

Figure 1

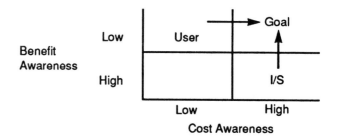

CONCLUSION

We sweep too many items under the rug with the statement, "You can't measure it." Management is tired of hearing words like, "We've got to do it in order to survive" or "It has key strategic impact." I like a thought process that can connect these kinds of statements to a bottom line expression. Even if the degree of certainty is low, the process itself can be enlightening and may serve to bring a perspective to a project that might otherwise roll through the approval cycle on the rhetoric of an articulate spokesperson.

To avoid this "hype," I contend that quantifiable estimates of intangible benefits can realistically be used to measure the return on investment of strategic systems — the same approach used to measure other capital expenditures. Thus, the new computer economics in reality may be a more intelligent and realistic employment of the old economics.

REFERENCES

1. Wiseman, Charles, *Strategy & Computers: Information Systems as Competitive Weapons,* Dow Jones-Irwin, Homewood, Illinois, 1985.
2. Rockart, John, "The CEO Goes On-line," *Harvard Business Review,* January-February 1982.

3. Vitale, Michael, Professor, Harvard Business School, in a speech given at Honeywell Executive Conference, Boston, May 1986.
4. Porter, M.E., Millar, V.C., "How Information Gives you Competitive Advantage," *Harvard Business Review,* July–August, 1986.

ABOUT THE AUTHOR

Jerry Kanter is the Director of Babson College's Center for Information Management Studies, a cooperative effort of business and academia to improve the use of information systems. Prior to starting the Center, Jerry served in a wide variety of information systems management and technical positions at the Honeywell Company in Boston, and at the Kroger Company in Cincinnati. His most recent position was as a consultant where he specialized in information systems planning, end-user computing, and organizational issues.

Prentice-Hall has published five of his books, the latest being Computer Essays for Management, *in 1987. His book* Management Information Systems, *is used as a standard text in many universities. He has also written many articles for professional journals and has lectured at schools such as Harvard, Dartmouth, Baylor, Northwestern, and Oxford and Cambridge in England. He is a frequent speaker at information systems conferences.*

Jerry is a graduate of Harvard College and the Harvard Business School.

THE INFORMATION SPIRAL: TOWARD A NEW PARADIGM FOR INFORMATION MANAGEMENT

Louann K. Reilly

Our current information management paradigm is insufficient to transition us from an industrial society to an information-based society. Changes in our information management practices consistent with a new, holistic management paradigm are key to successful competition in the Information Age. This article pulls together a variety of sources to integrate a set of ideas on what constitutes the art of information management in an information-based society. Particular attention is given to how Information Managers can promote and enable market-based management.

Innovation and the creation of new paradigms herald the coming of any new age. Anticipation of the Information Age is spawning new visions of a future in which information linked with new technologies will augment or replace many of the activities and services that characterize today's society. As we continue on a spiral flight toward full realization of the Information Age, a new paradigm for information management is evolving. It's evolution is in parallel with the management changes we are witnessing in other disciplines, including business, technology, health, and organizational behavior.

The shift to a new information management paradigm will occur with the recognition that our current information management paradigm, born of the industrial age, is insufficient to transition us from an industrial society to an information-based society. Changes in the goal of information management and its underlying assumptions will accompany the shift. Actualization of the new paradigm will require changes in our information management practices, changes that we can take action steps toward today.

MANAGEMENT PARADIGM FOR THE INDUSTRIAL AGE

An excellent discussion of changes in our management paradigm is offered in "Characteristics of Managers of the Future," a presentation by mental health expert F. Theodore Reid, delivered to The Dooley Group's 6th Annual Executive Conference (December 8, 1987, in Phoenix, Arizona). Reid describes the underlying paradigm of the scientific revolution and the industrial age as a Newtonian paradigm. The machine was the ultimate model. Deductive reasoning, with information gained by splitting a subject into its component parts and further analyzing each part, was the key to increasing knowledge. Reid points out that the mark of the Newtonian paradigm is evident in many disciplines, in physics — with emphasis on the atom and its component parts as the basic machine; in medicine — with the view of the human body as the ultimate machine; and in management theory — as reflected in productivity and time-motion studies. It is especially evident in the birth and development of data processing.

The computer has become the business world's ultimate machine. In the early days of data processing, the industry vernacular was hardware-based, speaking of *computer* systems, *computer* security, *computer* programmers. Over time, market demand fueled by advancements in technology contributed to a shift in focus from computer systems and data to management information systems and decision support information; from centralized mainframe computers to distributed processing on microcomputers; from flat files to database management systems; from database administration to data administration. The computer/data processing industry has become the computing/information processing industry.

In the evolution of information science, we can see advancements made based on utilization of the Newtonian paradigm. The practice of normalization (breaking down data into its most elementary components) and the use of relational theory in database management systems (DBMS) exemplify application of the paradigm to data management.

The more recent concept of asset management as applied to database and system design also is born of this paradigm. Data is viewed as a corporate asset which should be managed as such, analogous to the corporate controller's management of financial assets. Systems are engineered from component pieces, or modules, many of which are reusable from one system to another and thus can be developed as assets. Successful uses of relational technology and asset management demonstrate the continued utility of the traditional information processing paradigm in resolving *some* information management problems.

EVOLUTION OF A NEW PARADIGM

Continuing with the observations made by Reid, however, the implications are that a new paradigm for how we learn is evolving as new, different problems surface that cannot be resolved by further analysis under the microscope. Today's problems of integration and hyperextension (more services faster) are better suited to inductive than deductive reasoning for their resolution. Understanding cross-unit dependencies and the interrelationships of forces and entities in the universe is the new key to knowledge gain. The theory of holism is implicitly bound in the new paradigm — there is more to the whole than the sum of its parts. A shift toward a holistic paradigm is evident in the physical sciences — from Newton's theories to Einstein's; in medicine — with the move toward holistic approaches to healing; and in organization theory — with the concept of the extended enterprise.

Instead of being linked to any one industry, many companies today have a primary industry association but operate in multiple competitive sectors. They operate in an economy that places a premium on added value and responsiveness. As expressed by Mitchell Fromstein, President and CEO of Manpower Temporary Services, the effectiveness of the extended enterprise depends on the ability to assess all existing and potential relationships the company is party to, and to then efficiently capture, manipulate, and exchange information pertaining to those relationships. ("IBM Directions," June 1988) There is increasing recognition that effective strategy development requires reconciling multiple dimensions: how to add value, what products to offer, with whom to compete or form an alliance, and why — to play what game, to follow what strategic direction. The need for knowledge that will enable a company to reduce the cost and increase the effectiveness of all of its strategic relationships, and to reconcile multiple strategic dimensions, has given rise to the demand for integrated knowledge bases and inter-organization systems (IOS).

An information processing paradigm is a microcosmic image of the underlying paradigm for how we as humans learn about our universe. As Reid noted in his study of paradigms, the implications abound that in information management we are between paradigms. We are still solving problems in information processing with the old paradigm, but the growing interest in information systems architecture reflects the fact that there are problems we face which call for an integrative, holistic approach to their resolution. Perhaps the most important implication is the changing definition of what constitutes information management.

A MODEL FOR INFORMATION MANAGEMENT

In an industrial society, a basic view of the economic model of supply and demand lends itself well to the management of data. Drawing upon the writings of Daniel A. Appleton, specifically his article entitled "Information Asset Management" (*Datamation*, February 1, 1988), supply equates to raw (atomic) data and the technology for processing it. Demand equates to the product delivered to the user of information, typically derived data. Management attention is focused on the supply side, and specifically, the technology.

In our transitional stage between an industrial and an information-based society, Appleton directs management attention toward understanding the transactional relationships between supply and demand. Application of an economic model must be used with caution, however, for it is important to recognize the distinctiveness of information as an asset. Information is a logical asset that is subject to entropy but cannot be depleted in the sense that a corporation's physical assets — financial, human resource, machinery — can. The appreciation and depreciation value of information assets is highly specific and variable. The holistic paradigm teaches us that the symbiotic relationships of information supply and demand may be more instructional than the transactional ones. Supply and demand are closely intertwined along the pathway of transformation from data to knowledge.

Management scholar Ikujiro Nonaka, in his article, "Toward Middle-Up-Down Management: Accelerating Information Creation," (*Sloan Management Review,* Spring 1988), expertly articulates the need for innovation and its relationship to a new paradigm for information management:

> *Organizations must not only process information, they must create it. . . . For innovation is not so much a process of gradually reducing uncertainty (processing information) in moving toward a prescribed goal. Rather, it is a process through which uncertainty is intentionally* increased *when circumstances demand the generation of chaos from which new meaning can be created. . . . The quality of information becomes more important than the quantity. Inductive, synthetic, holistic methodologies become more useful than the deductive, analytic, and reductionist ones used in information processing.*

Information management thus constitutes not only information processing, but information creation. The focus is on the quality of information, or more succinctly, *the ability to transform information into knowledge.*

In an Information Age, Nonaka points out that market demand is for knowledge, intuitive knowledge as well as overt. Supply equates to individual-directed data flow, i.e., information precisely focused to meet the individual (or market) need to use knowledge as the agent for beneficial action. The development within computer and information sciences of concepts such as I-CASE (*Integrated Computer Aided Software Engineering*), knowledge bases, artificial intelligence, object-oriented processing, and neural networks demonstrate a holistic approach to information processing consistent with the new paradigm, and consistent with the increasing sophistication of market demand.

CHANGING ASSUMPTIONS

A long-held assumption underlying information management is that information services or MIS organizations have primary responsibility for the management of data. The concept of business ownership of data revolves around the issue of control. The assumption is that a well-managed data resource is one that is closely controlled and economically supplied. Information management planning activities reflect this supply-side emphasis. The goal: stable data resources.

A new paradigm for information management forces a challenge of these inveterate assumptions. Consider instead the assumption that a well-managed data resource is one that flows with a minimum of discrimination, to further stimulate information creation. Consider business data ownership being defined as accountability for the dynamics of the data resource — its development and investment potential,

Figure 1. The information spiral.

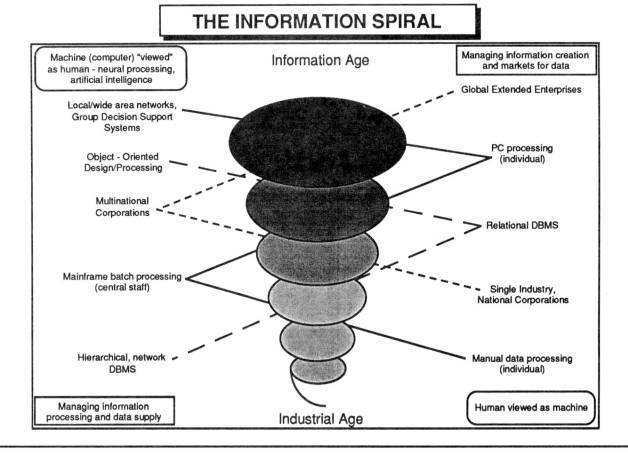

its value-adding potential, its directed flow — as opposed to its stabilization and control. Consider assigning stewardship of data within an organization based not on which functional area creates the data but, instead, which functional area stands to gain (or lose) most from use (or misuse) of the data. The goal is to help the organization to learn, to have the ability to create and apply knowledge to produce a desired business result.

We cannot achieve our future goal by an incremental improvement of our current information management practices. The difference in assumption sets is too extreme for evolutionary reformation. This is true of any paradigm change, and is illustrated in the following description of the management challenge in the manufacturing environment:

Today, however, companies are beginning to realize that they need something more than caretakers or specialists. They need generalists — people with an architect's skill, who can pull out a fresh sheet of paper and design something new.

It is not easy, however, to convert caretakers into architects. It takes a long period of training, of trial and error — new expectations and new rewards. It probably will also require new people, people like the giants of the first half of this century who established most of the perfectly reasonable — but now failing — manufacturing infrastructure common today." (Robert H. Hayes and Ramchandran Jaikumar, "Manufacturing's Crisis: New Technologies, Obsolete Organizations, Harvard Business Review, September–October 1988, Number 5, p. 85)

The information manager, then, must make the leap from caretaker to architect, from administrator to business leader, from the back office to the front line.

IMPLICATIONS FOR INFORMATION MANAGEMENT

The most important challenge for information managers is how to help the business organization create and apply knowledge to its competitive advantage. The quest for competitive advantage for many companies translates into the need to be market driven. Examination, then, of how information managers can promote and enable market-based management, deserves particular attention.

Central to the concept of being market driven is that a company understands *and acts upon* the buying influences and habits of its customers. To do so, customer information must flow beyond sales and marketing functions. In an article entitled, "What The Hell is 'Market-Oriented'?" (*Harvard Business Review,* November–December 1988, Volume 66, Number 6), Harvard Business School Professor Benson Shapiro elaborates on the importance of customer information permeating every corporate function, influencing both the input to and results of those functions. In a certain sense, there exists within the business organization a "market" for customer information, as business functional areas need customer information to identify and satisfy the product/service needs of the external marketplace. The implications for the information management function of a company striving to be market driven is to focus on managing this "market" for customer information. The focus is two fold: the creation of customer information and the infusion of customer information into the activities of every corporate function.

The identification of opportunities to create customer information within an organization may require a new perspective of the role that business functions and/or technology play in an organization. One such example is the use of an organization's sales force as a marketing intelligence system. This example is provided by Troy A. Ferstervand, Stephen J. Grove, and R. Eric Reidenbach in their article, "The Sales Force as a Marketing Intelligence System," (*The Journal of Business and Industry Marketing,* Volume 3, Number 1, Winter 1988). The authors describe the scenario as follows:

Sales people, based on their access to the marketplace, have the unique opportunity to monitor and report shifts in customer needs and competitive activity to marketing management. This can be done with little sacrifice of their own management productivity (selling time). In most organizations this opportunity remains untapped, largely due to reward systems which fail to provide incentives for this type of intelligence gathering activity.

The information manager, in uncovering opportunities for customer information creation, can serve as a catalyst for change within the organization, enabling it to take advantage of these opportunities and become more market driven.

To facilitate the infusion of customer information into every corporate function, information managers must understand what customer information adds value to the results of which business activities, and how it adds value. How do the business functional areas use customer information? In what way can customer information contribute to the successful achievement of the organization's key strategies and objectives? What customer information does the organization currently have "in inventory" and how efficiently and effectively is it used in meeting the business need to be market driven?

The challenge to information managers and providers of information services/processing is to practice market-based management of data, to manage data from the perspective of an agent for the buyer, the "buyer" being the user of information; to architect (and not just be a caretaker for) the data and systems required to satisfy knowledge demands. The concept of customer information being "owned" by the sales or marketing division within an organization runs counter to the demands of a market-driven company. Instead, accountability must be assigned within the organization for managing the "market" for customer information, for satisfying the customer information needs of all functions and divisions effectively and efficiently. Accountability implies control of the information resource; experience has shown us that the reverse is not necessarily true.

Figure 2. Market-based management: changing our view of the pyramid.

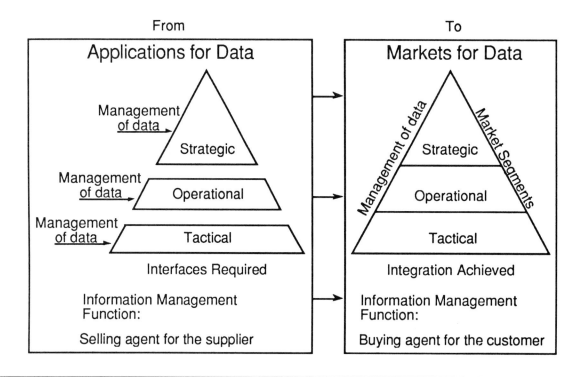

MANAGING INTERNAL INFORMATION MARKETS: WHERE TO BEGIN?

The practice of managing internal markets for information should parallel that of managing external markets for goods and services; that is, many of the same basic functions should be performed, from market research to service provision. What must be done first? Put someone in charge! Executive management must assign accountability to market managers for meeting the organization's needs for critical information. They must establish new performance measurements which reward the creation and distribution of information that enables the corporation to provide superior service to customers. And, as always, they must allocate the necessary resources to get the job done.

Consider the following example of what functions would be performed when managing an internal market for customer information:

- Market Research & Analysis
  - Assess the environment: assess the corporation's current and future needs for customer data, its use of emerging technologies and how that use might influence information requirements and availability, legislative/regulatory constraints regarding the data, and demographic trends that might indicate changes in the data and/or its availability.
  - Define target market(s): identify the functions and organizations within the corporation that use or create customer data.

- Gather intelligence about and analyze competitors' use of customer data.

- Market Plan Development and Implementation
  - Identify new and expanded opportunities for internal use *and creation* of customer data; determine the investment required to pursue such opportunities and the associated risk/gain potential.
  - Develop target market segment plans: plan how to enable/reward the creation of valuable customer data and how to satisfy the customer information requirements of internal functions and organizations.
  - Track market plans and evaluate the contribution of information management to the corporation's economic and strategic performance (through satisfaction of the demand for customer information).

- Information Asset Development
  - Monitor the creation of customer data models and the design and engineering of customer databases and customer data creation/delivery systems.

- Information Asset Delivery
  - Develop customer databases/systems distribution strategies.
  - Negotiate opportunities for customer data creation; negotiate access to customer information.
  - Track projects concerned with customer information assets.
  - Oversee the implementation of customer databases and manage vendor performance.

- Service
  - Establish and conduct communication programs which promote value-adding uses of customer information assets.
  - Provide assistance to the creators/users of customer information (handle inquiries, resolve interface problems, etc.).

An information market manager's guiding axiom: information about a business entity (customer, vendor, product, etc.) is as important as the entity itself.

CHANGES IN INFORMATION MANAGEMENT PRACTICES

Today, companies are recognizing the need for new organizational and managerial structures in order to be more responsive to a fluid marketplace, structures which promote interfunctional and interdivisional communication and decisionmaking. These new structures and the goal they support call for profound changes in information management practices.

ONE — Focus on Opportunities to Create Information Within an Organization

As previously mentioned, the identification of opportunities for information creation may require a new perspective of the role that business functions and technology play in an organization. Use of the sales force as a marketing intelligence system is one example.

The manufacturing environment provides another example. In their previously noted article, Hayes and Jaikumar point out that manufacturing technology creates and processes information as well as materials. The technology can become a powerful means for enhancing knowledge if the information it creates is used to full advantage.

TWO — Embrace the Heterogeneous and Dynamic Information Environment

Effective information management in a dynamic environment requires an emphasis on flexibility more than stability. The focus is not on rigid standardization of data (everyone speaks the same language) but on relating data (one language can be effectively translated to another, without loss of semantic integrity). In the computing environment, many Chief Information Officers (CIOs) are shifting their attention from controlling computing power to focusing on the networks that connect them. This shift reflects the fact that today's problems of data integration and accessibility are primarily problems of information creation and communication (networking) rather than of traditional information processing.

THREE — Reconcile Multiple Dimensions in the Formulation of Information Management Strategies

An effective information management strategy is a harmony of three key dimensions: business entities, business functions, and business relationships.

1. **Business entities.** A business entity is a person, place, thing, or event which is integral to the business's organization and activities. Primary examples are customer, product, and supplier. Information management along the business entity dimension focuses on satisfying the organization's information needs relative to a particular entity. Managing the "market" for customer information across business functions and divisions is an example of the business entity dimension.

2. **Business functional needs.** Management of data along the dimension of business functional need requires the identification of what information is required to perform specific business functions. The information requirements may span multiple business entities. Subsequent decisions regarding investment in information resources are guided by (1) the relative importance of the business function in meeting the organization's objectives, and (2) the relative importance of the information requirement (information on a business entity) to performance of the function.

   Business modeling concepts, and value-chain analysis or similar methodologies (e.g., strategy/information matrices) lend themselves well to the process of managing information in accordance with business functional need.

3. **Business strategic relationships.** A business is party to various relationships — with customers, suppliers, unions, venture partners, etc. This dimension of information management focuses on what information is needed to decrease the cost and increase the effectiveness of each of these relationships. The relationships are weighted according to their strategic importance and the information requirements for those relationships are prioritized according to the value they add, similar to the analysis performed from the business functional need perspective.

FOUR — Simplify; Be Precise

A key information leadership skill is the ability to synthesize the complexities of today's business and information processing environment to create an adaptable, simplistic framework for information management practices in the future.

Concentration on no more than a few clear, unifying, business objectives provides the precise focus necessary to ensure effective information management practices by autonomous operating units. Peter Drucker illustrates this point in his article, "The Coming of the New Organization," (*Harvard Business Review,* January–February 1988, Number 1), by using the analogy of a symphony:

> *There are probably few orchestra conductors who could coax even one note out of a French horn, let alone show the horn player how to do it. But the conductor can focus the horn player's skill and knowledge on the musicians' joint performance... The challenge that management faces is giving its organization of specialists a common vision, a view of the whole.*

FIVE — Change the Measures of Success and Rewards

The value of our information resources and the return on investment in these resources should be measured according to their contribution to the successful achievement of specific business objectives. For instance, investments for improvement of the accuracy of a specific set of data is of limited value if the value of the data to the organization is a function of its timeliness.

A suggested organizational response to operation of the information management function is the formation of business/technical partnerships, or coalitions, with shared performance measurement criteria. In other words, performance measures for information providers and information users alike for a given organization should support achievement of a single set of critical success factors.

This type of organizational approach is analogous to what Rosabeth Moss Kanter, the author of *The Change Masters,* describes as the "integrative organization." The integrative organization is formed by changing the relationships among various internal groups, e.g., product divisions, geographic divisions, and service units. Integration and collaboration become self-enforcing by making it necessary for each group to cooperate in order to achieve its own interests.

The integrative organization depends not so much on physical reorganization, but, as Kanter observes, on "creating a matrix in the minds of managers." It illustrates application of the holistic paradigm to organizational behavior.

THE INFORMATION SPIRAL

Much has been written about the need to find a balance between centralization and decentralization, between autonomy and control, between "market pull" and "technology push." In management, we have tended to view the shifts between these opposites as moving from one end of the pendulum to the other. The focus has been on narrowing the swing, on achieving equilibrium. But equilibrium, be it static or dynamic, does not connote forward movement.

In all probability we will continue to cycle between these opposing management forces. Our goal, however, is that these cyclical movements constitute an upward spiral, the advancement to higher levels of knowledge and subsequent action, accelerating us forward into the Information Age. Our resolve to take action steps today to implement a new, holistic information management paradigm is key. The degree to which we can learn about the interrelationships of forces and elements, and create based on that knowledge (such as the achievement of "market pull" and "technology push" through the coupling of accountability with leadership), will determine whether *we will indeed spiral toward success in the Information Age or lose our competitiveness by just going around in circles....*

BIBLIOGRAPHY

Appleton, Daniel S., articles on information management, specifically, "Information Asset Management," *Datamation,* February 1, 1988.

Barker, Joel A., *Discovering the Future: The Business of Paradigms,* ILI Press, 1986.

Bartlett, Christopher A. and Sumantra Ghoshal, "Managing Across Borders: New Organizational Responses," *Sloan Management Review,* Fall 1987, Volume 29, No. 1.

Carlyle, Ralph Emmett, "CIO: Misfit or Misnomer," *Datamation,* August 1, 1988.

Chorafas, Dimitris, "Is the Competition Ahead? Then Leapfrog Them," *Computerworld,* July 20, 1987.

Donovan, John J., "Beyond Chief Information Officer to Network Manager," *Harvard Business Review,* September–October 1988, Number 5.

Drucker, Peter F., "The Coming of the New Organization," *Harvard Business Review,* January–February, 1988, Number 1, and "Management and the World's Work," *Harvard Business Review,* September–October 1988, Number 5.

Ferstervand, Troy A., Stephen J. Grove, and R. Eric Reidenbach, "The Sales Force as a Marketing Intelligence System," *The Journal of Business and Industrial Marketing,* Volume 3, No. 1, Winter 1988.

Fredericks, Peter and N. Venkatraman, "The Rise of Strategy Support Systems," *Sloan Management Review,* Spring 1988.

Fromstein, Mitchell, as quoted in "IBM Directions," June 1988, pp. 3–4.

Gummessan, Evert, "Using Internal Marketing to Develop a New Culture: The Case of Ericsson Quality," *The Journal of Business and Industrial Marketing,* Volume 2, No. 3, Summer 1987.

Hayes, Robert H. and Ramchandran Jaikumar, "Manufacturing's Crisis: New Technologies,

Obsolete Organizations," *Harvard Business Review,* September–October 1988, Number 5.

Heldman, Robert K., *Telecommunications Management Planning: ISDN Network, Products, and Services,* TAB Books, Inc., 1987, Blue Ridge Summit, Pennsylvania.

Kanter, R. M., *The Change Masters* (New York: Simon & Schuster, 1983). As referenced in Barlett, Christopher A. and Sumantra Ghoshal, "Managing Across Borders: New Organizational Responses," *Sloan Management Review,* Fall 1987, Volume 29, No. 1.

Keen, Peter G. W., "Breakthroughs in the Organization," a presentation to the Yankee Group "Chief Information Officer: Teaming for Profit" conference, July 14–15, 1987, New York, NY.

Nonaka, Ikujiro, "Toward Middle-Up-Down Management: Accelerating Information Creation," *Sloan Management Review,* Spring 1988.

Reid, F. Theodore, "Characteristics of Managers of the Future," a presentation to The Dooley Group 6th Annual Executive Conference, December 8, 1987, Phoenix, Arizona.

Rouse, Robert A., "AI Is a Potential Total Change," a presentation to The Dooley Group 6th Annual Executive Conference, December 8, 1987, Phoenix, Arizona.

Shapiro, Benson P., "What the Hell Is 'Market Oriented'?" *Harvard Business Review,* November-December 1988, Number 6.

von Simson, Charles and Richard Layne, "Choice of a New Generation," *Information WEEK,* July 11, 1988.

ABOUT THE AUTHOR

Louann K. Reilly is a member of the technical staff at U S WEST Advanced Technologies, the research and development organization for U S WEST, Inc. Ms Reilly holds a B.A. from Ohio State University, and an M.A. from the Graduate School of International Studies, University of Denver. Her focus is on architecting an information infrastructure linked to enterprise-wide business strategy.

INFORMATION SYSTEMS: MESSAGES FROM THE PAST, LESSONS FOR THE FUTURE

Jerome Kanter

Because a service or product is possible doesn't insure it will be successful.

Videotext struggles and fails, struggles and fails. Only where it is given away and other competing services are withheld does videotext prosper.

The paperless office isn't. Paper is an especially convenient form for data transmission and has yet to be outlawed.

High tech with high touch was noted to be a needed combination for commercial and social acceptance technology. IBM's recent embrace of icons and mice signals another triumph of high touch. The news isn't new. Only the particular products which are flourishing or withering are new.

There is no question that in the Information Systems field we fall into the age-old trap of blithely ignoring the past while continually and enthusiastically pursuing the biggest, the best, and the brightest. In philosopher George Santayana's familiar words, "Those who do not remember the past are condemned to repeat it."

In this essay, I would like to discuss some of the technological and management developments that failed to become successes, at least up to the current time, and speculate why they did not make it, while at the same time other products were becoming commercial bonanzas. I use the term "speculate" because one has to conclude that there are many factors (timing and luck being among them) that comprise success, the composite of which is difficult if not impossible to measure. Then I will discuss the lessons learned from these experiences and the necessary actions to improve the odds of success in introducing new technology. These actions include recognizing information literacy as well as computer literacy, developing a new definition of "user friendly," discussing the need for "tweeners," that is, people who understand both the technology and the employment of it in different functional areas, and, finally, recommending a new approach for information systems curricula in business schools.

THE TWO-CULTURE MILIEU

A provocative framework was espoused by Sir C. P. Snow,[1] an English scientist whom I had the privilege of hearing in 1960 when he expressed his view of the "two-culture milieu" in the Godkin lecture series sponsored by Harvard University. Snow, trained in physics with a doctorate from Cambridge, was a prolific author with scientific books to his credit as well as over a dozen novels. He was knighted in 1957 and died in 1980. Like Winston Churchill, he was a man for many seasons.

Snow's basic thesis is that there has been a continued conflict throughout history between the scientist and the humanist. He referred, for example, to the decision in 1943 on strategic bombing in World War II, wherein the thinking was that bombing a city's population centers as well as its military and support centers would remove the will of the people to work and to resist. The thinking proved to be incorrect, as a study of post-war Germany by John Kenneth Galbraith showed that German war production went on rising until it reached its peak in August 1944. Snow used this issue to illustrate the danger inherent when a prime minister, in this case Winston Churchill, relies almost exclusively on a single scientific source (F. A. Lindemann) on which to base a complex decision with such far-reaching effects. He elaborated on the necessity for the humanist and scientist to reach the proper level of communication and understanding. The two-culture milieu has dangerous implications.

The two-culture milieu is most appropriate in reviewing the reasons products or product concepts work or don't work, because, like Sir C.P. Snow, I firmly believe a lack of the proper balance and consideration of both facets is the cause of success or failure. The two technologies or technological concepts under discussion are Videotext and the Paperless Office.

THE STAGNATION OF VIDEOTEXT

Videotext can be defined as the ability of individuals, within their home, to access information and information services via on-line telecommunications linkages to a variety of data sources. While this service is used extensively in England and in France, it has not caught on in the United States, epitomized by the demise of the Knight Ridder and Central Telephone ventures, to name just two. Currently IBM and Sears, through a joint venture called Trintex,[2] are planning to launch another version of Videotext based on access via a personal computer as opposed to access through a specialized terminal keyboard and the house television set, which were the previous approaches. The thinking is that people were not willing to pay the $600 to $900 which was the cost of the special terminal, but will be eager to use the service if they can tap in with their personal computer, which they already own.

To me, this is a prime example of a technological rather than a humanistic view of the world with dramatic financial implications for companies investing in the technology. The principal data services offered are news, business information, financial analysis, sports, weather, and, in general, the type of information available in the local newspaper. On-line ordering and access to a variety of public and private databases are also featured. The technology trappings to deliver this type of service into the home are definitely available and have been for some time.

The allure of this form of communication is the ability to specialize and personalize information to one's individual tastes. Thus, a news and sports profile can be developed to select those pieces of news that fit the predetermined profile, while automatically bypassing the myriad of events that one normally skips over in reading the daily newspaper. The "personalization" is one of the features Trintex feels will make the product it will call Prodigy such a big hit.

The major issue is that the buying habits, marketing motivation, and service propensities of the average consumer still favor the conventional delivery mechanisms. The confinement of a computer screen or even a television screen for receiving news is inferior to the mobility of the morning newspaper, which can be carried with you to the porch, den, or kitchen. And even the straightforward menu-driven instructions are to many an unnecessary communications layer. Likewise, shopping at the store or shopping mall provides a social or recreational activity that shopping at home can never substitute for. The electronic medium is still an inadequate and too impersonal alternate for ingesting news or making a buying decision. To this point, there are many who predicted the advent of video and optical disks would mark the end of movie theaters.

A counter argument to the lethargic Videotext market are those who say the situation will change with the new wave, the on-line generation who have become comfortable at an early age in using electronic means to communicate and access data. These are the people who subscribe to on-line bulletin boards and special-interest clubs, using them much like the CB radio. Each has his or her moniker (in this case, a password or ID number) and appreciates the impersonal mode of interaction as opposed to talking face to face. These are the citizens, so it is said, who will comprise the future Videotext market.

The widespread use of Videotext in France is a result of the fact that the nationalized French telephone company gives the terminal free to the household and it is the only way to look up a telephone number. There are no telephone books in France. Where there is competition for services, the Videotext alternative has not fared well. Videotext is a classic example of a technology in search of a market.

THE PAPERLESS OFFICE: WHITHER WENT THE REVOLUTION?

Remember the great cries that the use of word processors and the ability to file and store documents in electronic media would do away with the long rows of file cabinets and other office appurtenances dedicated to typing, copying, and physically exchanging documents? The fact of the matter is that there is more paper than ever, and the frantic concerns of the paper manufacturers over the paperless office and the aforementioned delivery of news via electronic means were, to pardon the expression, "paper tigers." It's widely known that the paper industry in the United States has been at or near capacity for a good number of years now.

The reasons for the premature prediction of the demise of paper has a similar sound to that of Videotext. It seemed logical that if you were able to access data from your terminal, there would be no need to have that same information on paper. Communication would be by electronic mail and documents could be retrieved and sent from one database to another where they could be accessed on a need-to-know basis. The paperless office pundits failed to recognize the convenience, portability and comfort level afforded by paper documents. The mindsets of businesspeople are linear in nature; that is, they are more comfortable with having their information in files in their desks, in folders on their desks, and in business reports in their hands, one page on top of the other. The interactive, browsing mode afforded by on-line data has not as yet been mastered even though there now are software systems on personal computers that begin to emulate the linear or sequential style of the businessperson. Most every user of electronic mail I know prints out their messages after they have read them on the screen.

Another dimension of the office environment has been the proliferation of desktop publishing. It has become very easy to produce documents that heretofore were the domain of professional publishers. The output looks great, and seemingly trivial stuff has a professional aura about it. As someone has said, "Nothing is quite as useless as doing with great efficiency that which shouldn't be done at all." This development has served as a counter-technological impact to the paperless office. It may prove to be as great a boon to the paper explosion as the electrostatic copier.

A development that promised to be another "winner" for an already dynamic and leading technological innovator was "Zap Mail," introduced by Federal Express[3] several years ago. It was a natural evolution for a communication company that was delivering over 750,000 information packets physically each day via their own fleet of aircraft, which each night converged in Memphis, Tennessee to sort out their cargo and send the multitude of reports and memos on their appointed rounds. One could have easily forecast that this was a "natural" to replace the physical effort of transporting paper by the transmission of electronic pulses over a telephone line or via satellite. Well, two years after initiating "Zap Mail," Federal Express junked the effort with a reported loss of $320 million. The reasons for the failure are manifold, but high on the list is people's propensity to want to see their original report delivered the next morning without electronic intervention rather than in the form of a facsimile copy. In effect, Federal Express's own efficiency built up an expectation and comfort level that made it difficult for their customers to adapt to a new process.

The penchant for paper documents brings back the days when accountants and financial analysts resisted the conversion of punched-card records to magnetic tapes. Somehow the ability to see physical holes in cards gave one a comfort level above that realized when one's critical data was represented in metallic oxide spots on a treated surface of tape, which were invisible to the naked eye. Today we are prepared to place our data into on-line disk storage, but we also want the paper output to carry in our briefcase and to place in our personal desk file.

WHAT DO THESE FAILURES TELL US?

There is no question that in order for a product to succeed it must be priced competitively and offer some unique features which could either be in the product itself or in the servicing of it. Also, it must be marketed and distributed effectively. All these things are obvious. The C. P. Snow framework presents another perspective from which to view product failures.

We must guard against being carried away with the technology and allowing the scientific partner to operate without the proper influence of the humanist. Another Englishman, Murray Laver, put it well when he said, "When we become overawed with technology, we become like the stereo enthusiast who, wild over woofers, intrigued with intermodulation, delirious over decibels and tantalized by tracking errors, comes to hate music."

Both Videotext and The Paperless Office developers failed to properly assess the behavior patterns of the ultimate users. A higher proclivity to adapt to the new media was assumed. As mentioned earlier, a popular belief today is that the new generation of college graduates will have been introduced to technology and computer usage such that it becomes embedded in the way they go about their work. The computer as a tool is a natural extension of their problem-solving ability. It will be used as an accountant uses an electronic spreadsheet. The proponents of this view would say that this new breed will be comfortable in the world of Videotext and The Paperless Office.

But there is a counter argument. The first wave of so-called computer-literate graduates have been on the scene for some time now. And what do you know? They operate as managers in the same way as their computer-illiterate predecessors. They think face-to-face contact is important, they feel on-line reporting and electronic mail, while useful in many areas, must be augmented by eye contact and body language, and they feel that too much introverted personal computer usage can get in the way of what's really important. And as consumers, the computer-literate still like to shop at the supermarket and the shopping mall and still obtain their news, sports, and weather via the local newspapers and television.

Despite the introduction of computers earlier and earlier in the schooling process, in elementary schools and even in nursery schools, there will continue to be a dichotomy of people and, to use C. P. Snow's terms, some will have a scientific aptitude while others will have a humanist one. The percentages may shift but not on a wholesale basis. Call it human nature or natural selection or whatever, it appears that this is the way people adapt and change.

This is not based on scientific evidence; it is a reflection based on observation and the behavior pattern of people during the industrial revolution and now the information era. While most businesspeople agree that significant scientific breakthroughs are observed in their commercial embodiment ten or more years after their discovery, similar changes of scope in human behavior take much longer.

LOOKING AHEAD: LESSONS FOR THE FUTURE

So where do we go from here? Keeping in mind the C. P. Snow reminder to blend the scientific view with the humanist view, what's going to happen in the world of Information Systems? I see the following lessons evolving from a review of past failures.

Information Literacy Is Different from Computer Literacy

There are two aspects or roles regarding information systems of which business managers must be aware. The first is as direct users themselves employing terminals in their offices to directly access information or using personal computers (PCs), also in their offices, to send electronic messages, maintain their calendars, or do spreadsheet calculations. The second role is that of directors of the use of information systems in the functions of the company over which they have responsibility. I have come to the conclusion that we have allowed our preoccupation with the first role to warp our perspective on the much more important second role.

I feel it is strictly a personal preference or management style that dictates whether a senior manager will be comfortable using a PC. There are left-brain (intuitive) managers and right-brain (structured, analytical) managers, and I think there will always be. It's also true that there's still a lot happening in the business world that can't be neatly plugged into the aseptic cells of spreadsheet. I still have a feeling that despite the progressively earlier introduction of PCs into the educational process, the left-brained will still represent the majority of tomorrow's CEOs and senior managers. John Deardon[4] has a point when he says a computer has not and will not have any important impact on the way a manager manages.

What I think important to business managers is not so much computer literacy but information literacy, the recognition that information is important, is of value, is an asset, and is a strategic commodity to a company. He must also realize the cost and energy that must be expended to capture, store, maintain, and communicate that data throughout the organization. He must have an "information perspective," to know when an information demand should be handled within minutes and when it's going to take years (to distinguish the trivial from the blockbuster); to know that he has to play a part in being able to use information strategically, that he has to be able to set priorities, place some sort of value on the information requested, and specify what he or his department really needs. A recognition of this is a key starting point for the development of systems concepts such as the Paperless Office and Videotext.

When One Speaks of User-friendly, Define the User

One of the most confusing but widespread terms in the information systems industry is user-friendly. We throw everything under that umbrella, an example being a function statement like "#Shift Key/*", which to a computer programmer is a user-friendly command, but would drive a business user up the wall and would send an executive searching for his Berlitz book on foreign languages. I always tell the story of my Boxer dog, Sammie. Sammie used to bite people's hands who visited the house, but I trained him and now he only nips at them. I call that user-friendly because I've seen the progress, but try to tell that to my friends. The analogy holds in human/computer interfaces, both in the office and in the home.

Information systems people sometimes have real difficulty when they develop executive systems. Most of the executives I know, and I don't mean this in a derogatory sense, have an attention span measured in microseconds. If they have to remember function keys or codes to get at information, no matter how useful it may be, they will not do it or at best get someone else to produce a report for them. It must be remembered that 80% of senior management are humanists, not scientists; paperless office proponents must keep this in mind.

There Is an Increasing Need for "Tweeners"

This is a word I have coined to classify the growing importance of a group of people who are the buffers, translators, facilitators, consultants, or whatever term you want to use. They are business trained, but are also comfortable with the technology. This indispensable group translates the needs of various layers of management into systems that concentrate on the "human factors." They operate by the dictum "elegance in simplicity" in that they are creative in shielding system complexity from the users of the system. They don't get their kicks out of designing a system that is unfathomable and so complex that only a nuclear physicist would feel comfortable using it.

In our educational and business institutions, these types of people have fallen in the cracks. The students majoring in computer science wind up programming and running the complicated mainframe transaction systems and the telecommunications networks of Fortune 1000 companies. The finance, marketing, and manufacturing majors go into the management of these line functions within the corporations of their choice. There are no training programs available for the important "tweeners." A new function is required which would call for a strong information systems background but in a context of understanding line business functions and human and organizational behavior.

From the company viewpoint, positions and growth paths should be provided (probably of the dual ladder variety) for these internal business information analysts. This can ensure that computers are used for their highest calling, that being their use in strategic areas of the business and in providing executives with information support for the things that are really important to them.

Modify the Role of Information Systems in Business Education

A nationwide phenomenon is occurring in the information systems education arena in colleges and universities. Enrollments in these courses are uniformly down throughout the country. A typical study is the one conducted at UCLA, which shows that freshman enrollment in computer careers dropped from its peak in 1982 of 8.8% to 3.5% in 1986.[5] With rare exceptions, this is a national pattern.

Several major direction changes are essential to refocus information systems education. For one, the scenarios established above must be considered. Though it has taken time, the advances in software and human interfaces are continuing to occur. The mouse-type input device, by which I am composing this essay, is a harbinger of what can happen. I look positively at voice recognition technology as a potential breakthrough for executive use of computer systems. Executives can "point," as in using the mouse, and they certainly can talk; what they won't do in the foreseeable future is type or key in esoteric codes. With these types of developments, more executives will become users themselves and will also be much more active in controlling their own infor_mation support systems. Also, Videotext systems using the new interface technology will be more attractive.

The education process must train managers for this type of usage. Information systems should be embedded within the regular functional disciplines like marketing and finance. The problem is that the teachers of these courses are not that familiar with computers and the information systems people are not that familiar with the functional areas. The solution could well be combination courses co-taught by IS professors and functional discipline professors. This would involve a collaboration and a sharing of the responsibility for curriculum development; the combination would be powerful and is already in practice at the institution where I work, Babson College. For example, a new course called Accounting Information Systems is now part of the Babson curriculum. This course, which is jointly given by Accounting and Information Systems professors, covers how Accounting Information Systems (i.e., general ledger, accounts receivable and payable) are controlled, maintained and, more important, are used to give a company a strategic advantage. Other such courses are offered or planned in Manufacturing, Marketing, and Finance. It follows the C. P. Snow philosophy of a proper meeting of minds between disciplines, between the scientist and humanist, in this case, the technologist and the functional manager.

CONCLUSION

The essay started by saying there were lessons to be learned from the past lest we repeat the mistakes. There is evidence to show we are well on the way of repeating the learning cycles of the mainframe and mini eras in this, the era of the personal computer. Thus we have, as Dick Nolan[6] has discovered, a proliferation phase occurring soon after the initiation of any new computer technology: a control phase ensues when the fragmented developments of the proliferation phase are halted and a concerned management begins to look at the expensive fragmentation that has occurred. A new stage develops as management and corporate information needs are more carefully assessed and integrated databases are built around a standard communication network required to connect the departments of a corporation. We seem to be repeating the Nolan stages with the introduction of systems concepts such as Videotext and the Paperless Office and the advent of personal computers.

Is it possible to learn from the past or do we have to systematically repeat the cycles with the accompanying vast expenditures of time, energy, and money? This essay has attempted to state some basic tenets that can minimize this transition. Enlightened mainframe information systems leaders, if this is not an example of a double oxymoron, are in the best position to assist in this transition. They have lived through the stages, and if they have developed a management proclivity in the process, can now act as business consultants to the new wave. Aside from that, the only course of action is to fall prey to the prophetic words of George Santayana.

REFERENCES

1. Snow, C.P., The Two Cultures: A Second Look, 2nd edition, Cambridge, England, Cambridge University Press, 1963
2. Saporito, Bill, "Are IBM and Sears Crazy? or Canny?" Fortune Magazine, September 28, 1987, p. 74-80.
3. Smith, Randall, "Federal Express, Minus Albatross, Still Faces Competition," Heard on the Street, Wall Street Journal, 1987
4. Deardon, John, "Will the Computer Change the Job of Top Management?" Sloam Management Review, Fall 1983, p. 57-60.
5. Rifkin, Glenn, "The Crisis in MIS Education," Computerworld, two-part article, June 15 and June 21, 1987.
6. Nolan, R.L., "Managing the Crisis in Data Processing," Harvard Business Review, Vol. 57, No. 2, 1979, p. 115-126.

ABOUT THE AUTHOR

Jerry Kanter is the Director of Babson College's Center for Information Management Studies, a cooperative effort of business and academia to improve the use of information systems. Prior to starting the Center, Jerry served in a wide variety of information systems management and technical positions at the Honeywell Company in Boston, and at the Kroger Company in Cincinnati. His most recent position was as a consultant where he specialized in information systems planning, end-user computing and organizational issues.

Prentice-Hall has published five of his books, the latest being Computer Essays for Management, *in 1987. His book* Management Information Systems, *is used as a standard text in many universities. He has also written many articles for professional journals and has lectured at schools such as Harvard, Dartmouth, Baylor, Northwestern, and Oxford and Cambridge in England. He is a frequent speaker at information systems conferences.*

Jerry is a graduate of Harvard College and the Harvard Business School.

AN EMERGING METHODOLOGY FOR MANAGING LARGE SYSTEMS PROJECTS

Robert C. Ford, Peter M. Ginter, Andrew C. Rucks, James B. Dilworth, J.W. Mitchell

Organizational rather than technical problems are cited as a common reason when project management fails. The use of a permanent, centralized project management group is suggested as a means to address information needs in large organizations. This paper reviews the customary role of project management in the traditional project life cycle and contrasts this with a three-stage model that provides a rationale for a permanent, centralized form of project management for large-scale organizations.

In the literature discussing project management, there is little discussion on how project management is integrated into the organizational design and structure. This lack is rather surprising since organizational rather than technical problems are commonly cited as the major reason for project management failure.[1,2] The omission of concern with the structural integration of project management has been traditionally viewed as a temporary phenomenon. Recently, however, "permanent, centralized project management" has emerged as a significant organizational structure for addressing the information needs of large organizations. The purpose of this paper is to review the traditional role of project management, examine the traditional project management life cycle, and provide evidence and rationale for a new project management organizational design appropriate to the "information age."

THE TRADITIONAL ROLE OF PROJECT MANAGEMENT

Project management techniques traditionally have been recommended for ad hoc undertakings, particularly when those undertakings are large-scale, unique, unfamiliar, or complex. Project management is used in organizations when "management gives emphasis and special attention to the conduct of nonrepetitive activities for the purpose of meeting a single set of goals".[3] In addition, project management has been viewed as providing a logical approach to managing the diverse efforts required in complex undertakings. In the traditional view, individual projects are not ongoing efforts, but rather have a definite beginning and ending. The management of a project requires that the project manager integrate the diverse functional and technical requirements of the project over this finite life cycle. Because of these attributes, the project management structure commonly has been used for information systems development which requires months or years to complete.

TRADITIONAL PROJECT MANAGEMENT LIFE CYCLE

The traditional view of the project management life cycle (PMLC) for information systems development is shown in Figure 1. It begins with the need for an information system recognized by some functional unit of the organization. This functional unit is often referred to as the "customer organization" or "user organization." Next, a proposal for an information

Figure 1. Traditional view of the project life cycle for information systems development.

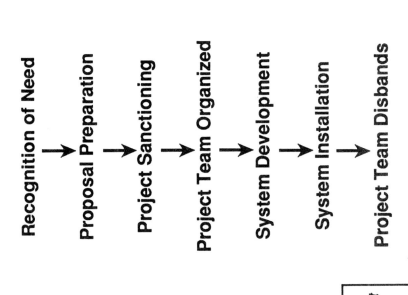

system project is developed and presented to a decision-making executive or council which can approve or disapprove the proposal. If the executive or council sanctions the project, a project manager is appointed from the customer organization. This position is typically a temporary duty assignment. The project manager usually has little prior project management experience and, therefore, obtains all such training through experience on the project itself. This manager, in turn, organizes a team to complete the assigned project. Thus, information systems development projects are typically decentralized and semiautonomous.

The traditional project team generally varies in size and composition during the course of the project. The project team acquires expertise from the functional areas of the organization as the need for expertise is required through temporary assignments of the functional experts. When a project team member's duties on the project are completed, the member returns to his or her department. Similarly, the manager returns to his or her functional or staff responsibilities. Because project team members are only temporarily assigned to the project and may never physically leave their home department, there is often a problem of dual loyalties and dual reporting responsibilities.

When the development stage is concluded, the product is installed for the customer. Following installation, the system is tested and evaluated to ensure that it functions properly in the "production" or customer environment. At the conclusion of testing and evaluation, the system becomes the property of the customer organization and the project team is dissolved. The responsibility of system maintenance, update, and problem solving for the information system is decentralized to the user at the completion of the project.

PROBLEMS WITH TRADITIONAL PROJECT MANAGEMENT

A major difficulty with the decentralized project management concept is the dual reporting structure of the matrix organization. In many cases, there is confusion when an employee has more than one boss. If, for example, a programmer is temporarily shared with a project team designing a complex decision-support system, and still maintains some of his or her former area of responsibility, the need to satisfy both the project manager and the regular boss may create considerable stress.

Dual reporting problems are compounded for members of the project team who never physically leave their work places while on temporary assignment. For instance, it takes a very disciplined boss to refrain from asking for help on a critical deadline from an employee temporarily assigned to a project team.

Similarly, it would take a very secure subordinate to not agree to help out even at the expense of project responsibilities.

The dual reporting responsibility problem and the murky authority problem of decentralized project management have created an entire literature on the personality profile best suited to project management leadership.[4] The project manager must be able to persuade functional managers to volunteer their best rather than worst people to staff the project team. In addition, the project manager has to excite, motivate, and lead a group of people who are assigned only temporarily to his or her unit and realize their career success more likely rests with their functional boss rather than the project manager.

In addition, the project manager needs to have the technical skills, managerial talent, and interpersonal ability to define a project, review and evaluate all possible alternatives available for project completion; and organize a temporary work force into a cohesive integrated organization. Although organizations in such environments occasionally find people who are able to accomplish projects, they are rare.

A NEW MODEL OF PROJECT MANAGEMENT FOR INFORMATION SYSTEMS DEVELOPMENT

The need for the concurrent development of several large information systems in many organizations has suggested some new perspectives concerning project management. These new perspectives have resulted in a departure from the traditional view of the project life cycle and project management's decentralized and temporary structure. For many organizations, it appears that a permanent and centralized structure may be the most appropriate for information systems development. The rationale for a new project management organizational structure may be found in examining the new realities of the information age.

The information age has spawned many "information systems dominant organizations" (ISDO) which process vast quantities of information. These organizations are involved in rapidly changing social and technological environments where user groups cannot be expected to stay abreast of important changes external to the organization. Moreover, such organizations have multiple users who often have interdependent or similar information requirements across organization lines. Finally, these organizations create "incremental systems" where improvements are continually being implemented. In this type of organization, complex systems are always under development and existing systems require at least periodic attention. For ISDO organizations, the traditional life cycle no longer is appropriate.

A Dynamic Three-stage Project Management Life Cycle

The model of a project life cycle presented in Figure 2 differs considerably from the traditional model presented in Figure 1 and reflects the need for a permanent and centralized project management organization. The model for information systems dominant organizations has only three stages: (1) product definition and approval, (2) product design and delivery, and (3) product maintenance and upgrade. The model is considered dynamic in the information systems dominant organization because each stage represents an ongoing requirement and a permanent organization has been created to accommodate project development

Since information systems development is commonplace in the ISDO, new information products are constantly in demand. Projects arise from one or a combination of three sources: user requests, nonuser requests that originate within the information systems organization, and external sources such as regulators. Once the product has been defined, schedules developed, and cost/benefits projected, it must meet with executive approval and funding.

In the second stage, the project team is formed; the project is designed, tested, and implemented; and the project team dissolved. Since systems development requests are common, the organization has a pool of project managers with project management experience and expertise available for directing projects. In addition, the project manager can view the project from the needs of the entire organization and thus ensure that the system to be developed is not redundant or overlapping with other systems.

In the last stage of the dynamic project management life cycle, the user has experience with the product and may request changes in the product, or the product may need to be upgraded to meet technological or regulatory developments. Further, the third stage of the model points to the importance of the completed life cycle and the inadequacy of the decentralized, traditional project management system to deal with this stage of project management. When the traditional, decentralized project team has finished the assignment, the usual pattern is to dissolve the team. At the point of divestment, the project-team members are repositioned in their former functional roles and the support resources assigned to the team reallocated. At that point, the user organization takes over the responsibility for operating the system delivered by the project team.

Traditional, decentralized project management does not address adequately the problem of monitoring the performance of the result of a project (product) to ensure that the product (1) continues to solve the problem for which it was created, (2) stays current with the applicable technology, (3) avoids overlapping responsibility with other parts of the organization, (4) continues resource sharing with other elements of the organization, and (5) meets availability and on-line response time required.

If the traditional, decentralized project management concept is inadequate for effectively coping with all but the middle stage of the project life cycle, what can be done to ensure that both the beginning and ending stages are adequately and completely addressed by the organization? The answer is to centralize the project management function and constitute it as a permanent, ongoing organizational unit.

Figure 2. Project management life cycle.

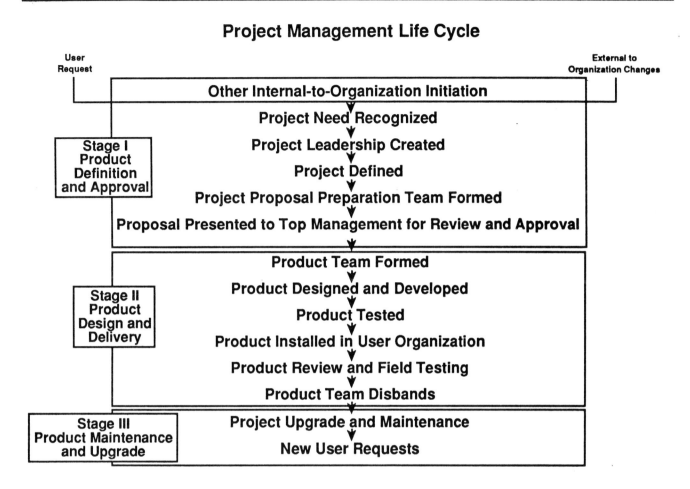

Permanent, Centralized Project Management at BellSouth Corporation

To illustrate the usefulness of the relatively unexplored role a permanent centralized approach to project management may play and how this organizational structure fully addresses the entire project management life cycle, the experiences of the Information System Services (ISS) organization of BellSouth Services, Inc. will be examined. BellSouth Services' ISS is an excellent illustration of centralized project management. BellSouth Services developed this structure because it is a large organization that does business in a rapidly changing environment, has multiple users for its products, and is frequently assigned responsibility for incremental changes in a product after development.

BellSouth Services is a division of BellSouth Corporation, one of the seven regional holding companies created by the 1984 divestiture of American Telephone and Telegraph (AT&T). BellSouth is the holding company for two telephone operating companies — South Central Bell (serving Alabama, Kentucky, Louisiana, Mississippi, and Tennessee) and Southern Bell (serving Florida, Georgia, North Carolina, and South Carolina). These two operating companies jointly own BellSouth Services, which provides support services to both operating companies. Information System Services (ISS) coordinates project management for systems development for BellSouth, Inc. These relationships are shown in the organization chart presented in Figure 3.

Information System Services has responsibility for the installation and operation of most of the computer-based systems used by the operating companies. Under the coordination of ISS, each phase in the project life cycle is performed through centrally managed interdepartmental project teams. These teams include a planning team, design team, implementation team, and operations team. Each team is headed by a professional project manager who is a member of the ISS staff. The teams have significant user involvement for the accomplishment of their missions, and it is the responsibility of the project manager to identify the need for user involvement and integrate the user into the system development process. The project manager is in a position of leadership. The primary focus of this leadership is to direct the project in such a way that the user is assured that the information system being developed meets his or her needs. The project manager leads the user in system specification and leads the system developers to meet user expectation.

The commitment to user involvement is further reinforced by the project manager recruitment practices of ISS. ISS selects members of its professional project management staff on the basis of their user expertise rather than systems/technology expertise. This practice is based on the philosophy that it is easier to teach a project manager systems or technology than user understanding.

The Scope of Permanent Centralized Project Management

The ISS approach, as demonstrated by the management of projects for South Central Bell, involves the establishment of a specialized and permanent organization dedicated to systems planning, design, implementation, and operation. The commitment to professional project management is supported by the fact that project management is a significant part of the assignments of three of the six assistant vice presidents within ISS.

In the ISS approach, a Planning Team is responsible for developing the project proposal and produces the approval documents for a project. Once this task is completed, the project planning organization (which may be a project manager and an informal organization or a formal project organization) dissolves. This dissolution of the project planning organization simply means that the project manager is available to focus on the planning of another project.

Upon approval, the design team performs its role of system design. The design team is responsible for developing detailed systems configurations, determining system components, developing interfaces among systems, and creating design specifications. The implementation team is responsible for obtaining hardware and software, implementing work flows, and converting databases. The operations team performs maintenance or enhancements and identifies and corrects deficiencies.

Perhaps one of the most significant features of project development is the project recycling feature.

Figure 3. BellSouth Corporation and principal subsidiaries.

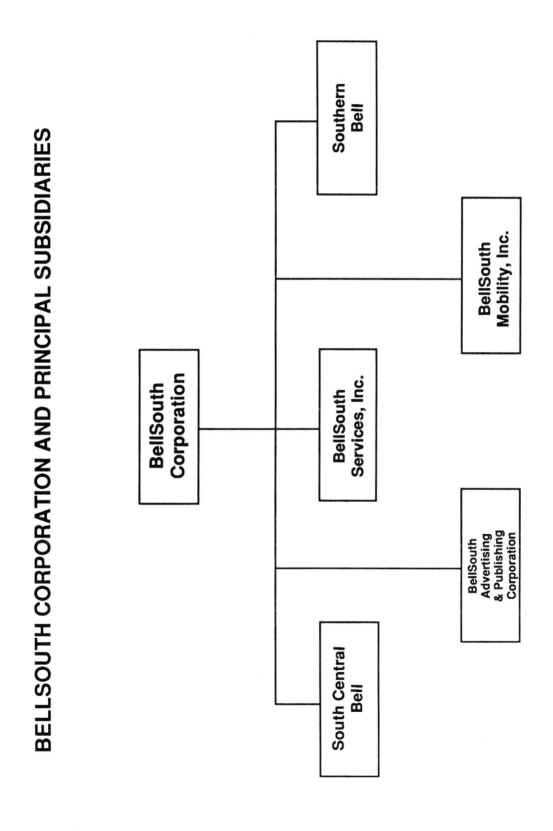

At any stage of the life cycle, a project may be referred to the previous team that worked on it for alterations. The idea underlying this referral is to prevent system problems from becoming a permanent part of a system.

Advantages of Permanent Centralized Project Management

The permanent centralized project management structure, such as that used by ISS, has several important advantages for the large organization with many interrelated and diverse system needs. Many of these advantages may be realized only by sufficiently large organizations operating in a technologically complex and rapidly changing product environment. The advantages of centralized project management experienced by BellSouth Services Company include the following items.

1. Centralized project management reduces the overall size of the organization by eliminating the need for user organizations to maintain spare personnel that can be used as project managers.
2. Centralized project management guarantees the availability of well-trained, experienced project managers. Therefore, the beginning-of-project lag that often arises because a project manager, selected from the user organization, may not possess project coordination skills is eliminated. For example, personnel from user departments may not be familiar with ad hoc budgeting, scheduling, or the procedures for developing and managing a project team. With centralized project management, projects are managed by professional, experienced project managers. Additionally, the inclusion of a project management function in the organizational structure creates a career path for persons specializing in the management of projects. Such an organization creates a pool of experienced project managers capable of assuming project management for any type of system.
3. Centralized project management fosters the development and maintenance of documentation and system-interface standards. User departments typically do not have knowledge of or adhere to system documentation and interface standards. However, in centralized project management, the user receives centralized support following installation of a system. The user returns to the project management organization for support and modification of systems.
4. Centralized project management guarantees the integration of information systems throughout the corporation. User departments may have no knowledge of the needs of other departments and therefore often fail to integrate their systems into those of the organization as a whole. A centralized project management organization is in a better position than the dispersed users to establish system priorities and identify possible overlaps. In addition, the centralization of developmental priorities facilitates the integration of all systems into the total system organizational plan and helps to eliminate the problems when one system duplicates the work of an existing system.
5. Centralized project managers do not exhibit a split loyalty between a project and a functional unit. Project managers, under the decentralized approach, know that when their time on the project ends, they will return to their functional unit. Therefore, they attempt to optimize the returns to corporate requirements.

SUMMARY

Using the South Central Bell illustration, the usefulness of the centralized permanent project organization in ensuring adequate and effective coverage of stages one and three in the project life cycle was addressed. While the traditional focus of project management stresses decentralized structure, the illustration used here indicates that only in the stage-two aspects of the project life cycle is there a substantive argument for a decentralized system for implementing project management.

FOOTNOTES

1. Butler, Arthur G., Jr., "Project Management: A Study in Organizational Conflict," *Academy of*

Management Journal, 16:1, March 1973, 84–101.
2. Cleland, David I. and William R. King, *Systems Analysis and Project Management,* New York: McGraw-Hill Book Company, 3rd Edition, 1983.
3. Conway, McKinley, "A New Wave of Super Projects?" *Industrial Development,* May/June 1983, 4–9.
4. Fulmer, Robert M., "Product Management: Panacea or Pandora's Box," *California Management Review,* Summer 1965.

BIBLIOGRAPHY

DeMaagd, Gerald R., "The Psychology of Project Organization," *Managerial Accounting,* September 1983, 10+.

Felix, Robert C. and William L. Harrisen, "Distributed Processing Application Success," *Management Information Systems* Quarterly, Vol. ___, September 1984, 161–170.

Galbraith, Jay R., "Matrix Organization Design," *Business Horizons,* 1971, 14 (1), 29–40.

Katz, Ralph and Michael L. Tushman, "A Longitudinal Study of the Effects of Boundary Spanning Supervision on Turnover and Promotion in Research and Development," *Academy of Management Journal,* Vol. 26, 1983, 437–456.

Kolodny, Henry F., "Evolution to a Matrix Organization," *Academy of Management Quarterly,* Vol. 3, No. 3, September 1977, p. 27.

Potts, Paul, "Project Management: Getting Started," *Journal of Systems Management,* February 1982a, 18–19.

Potts, Paul, "Project Manager: Technician or Administrator," *Journal of Systems Management,* January 1982b, 36–37.

Robb, Russell, "Lectures on Organization," Graduate School of Business Administration, Harvard University, 1910.

Shanks, Jack G., "Managing Projects Requires Four Main Ingredients," *Data Management,* December 1983, 14–15+.

Thamhain, H. J. and D. L. Wilemon, "Conflict Management in Project Life Cycles," *Sloan Management Review,* Summer 1975, 31–50.

Wall, William C., Jr., "Integrated Management in Matrix Organization," *IEEE Transactions on Engineering Management,* Vol. EM–31, February 1984, 30–36.

White, K. B., "MIS Project Teams: An Investigation of Cognitive Style Implications," *Management Information Systems Quarterly,* June 1984, 95–101.

Wolff, Michael F., "Managers at Work: When Projects Select You (Or the Researcher as Firefighter)," *Research Management,* May/June, 1983, 8–9.

Zachery, William B. and Robert M. Krone, "Managing Creative Individuals in High-Technology Research Projects," *IEEE Transactions on Engineering Management,* February 1984, 37–40.

ABOUT THE AUTHORS

Peter M. Ginter *(Ph.D., University of North Texas); Professor of Management in the Graduate School of Management at the University of Alabama at Birmingham (UAB). Ginter is a specialist in strategic planning and decisionmaking. He was previously on the faculty of the University of Arkansas, and worked in the telecommunications industry. He is the author of four books, and numerous articles and papers on management strategy. Ginter is past president of the Southwestern Federation of Administrative Disciplines. He is a frequent consultant to organizations in the southeastern United States.*

Andrew C. Rucks *(Ph.D., University of North Texas); Professor of Information Systems and Associate Dean of the School of Business, Samford University. Rucks previously held the position of Director of Computer and Telecommunication Services at Samford University. Prior to joining Samford in 1987, Rucks was on the faculties of UAB, the University of Arkansas, and Auburn University. Rucks is the author of two books and specializes in* computer and telecommunication systems design and installation. Rucks consults with local, regional, and national organizations. Rucks' current interest is information systems.

James B. Dilworth *(Ph.D., Arizona State University); Professor of Management in the Graduate School of Management at the University of Alabama at Birmingham (UAB). Ford is the author or co-author of two books on management and organizational theory, and numerous articles on a variety of managerial issues which are published in both theoretical and practitioner journals. He is a member of the research committee for the Society for Human Resources Management, and the past chair of the Management Education and Development Division of the Academy of Management.*

Jay W. Mitchell *(B.A., M.A., University of Alabama); Adjunct professor at University of Alabama, Birmingham (UAB). Mitchell has close to 40 years' experience as vice president with Southern Bell, South Central Bell, and BellSouth in staff and operational areas such as information systems, corporate plans and services, information resources, corporate support and procurement, property, and service. He was founding president of the Alabama Society for Information Management and is a member of SIM and other professional and civic organizations.*

THE ART OF MANAGING UPWARD

Richard E. Dooley

Managing subordinates is supposed to be a very challenging task. Managers continually are told that they don't do a very good job of it and are intimidated by numerous surveys and circumstantial evidence of their failings.

Managing those who don't directly report to you is even more difficult. We often call this task project management or matrix management. The current literature acknowledges that this is a legitimate field of study, but like the Sasquatch or Bigfoot, at best we know someone who has actually seen one (either a Bigfoot or successful project manager).

But our success hinges on how well we manage our bosses and those others around us who actually make the difference in our being effective or not and who also keep score on our effectiveness. Hardly anyone studies this task of "managing up." Even fewer write about it.

Most of us initially perceived, and then began learning, the management process with a heavy bias towards the idea of managing subordinates only. Managers managed down from their position whether that position was organizational or experiential. We ourselves had been managed — by parents, by teachers, by supervisors — and there was a strong sense of "It's done unto us, from above," so it was natural to assume our management focus would continue in the same direction.

Actually there are six directions in which the management process must move effectively:

1. **Upward** — We all have bosses of one kind or another and will forever. They always require interaction and usually welcome influence. This view is the focus of this article.
2. **Downward** — This is the traditional, perhaps most visible and most practiced view.
3. **Outward** — Managing to society, to the community, and to the global marketplace is more important than ever before.
4. **Inward** — To the self. Indeed, the most elusive. Not thought of as a "business process." Often assumed to be in place.
5. **Across** — Managing to and with peers, teammates, cohorts, within the greater organization but cutting across lines of responsibility or function.
6. **The Client** — To the customer, the final recipient of the service or product at hand.

The "switching gear" between the six directions is, of course, the aspiring individual who is learning the management process. All six are inextricably intertwined, which adds confusion and frustration to the eager student. After all, a manager is supposed to be in charge, right? It often seemed to me, the higher I rose in the organization and the more power I supposed I had, the less I was really in charge. I believe now that was because I was learning how deeply integrated these six directions really were, and how difficult was my job as the switching gear between them.

Despite an ultimate need to understand the combined thrust on us from all six, or from us into all six, directions, the direction from which the most visible influence, positive or negative, comes is above. Usually also, it is influence which cannot be avoided. So why not work cooperatively with it? The best managers have proactively harnessed the power above them in a living, synergistic way. It is possible for them to be much more effective because of that link no matter what they think of the value associated with what's above them.

I don't view this as being manipulative. For some it might seem so. Nor do I think of it as delegating upward, passing the buck, so to speak, which many are only too willing to do. I see this as a needed strength, a balancing or enhancing power, in any structure of people acting in the management process. So here are some suggested refinements for one of the six management directions (upward), although many of them can be applied to the other management directions also.

THE MEDIA/MEDIUM

First of all, bosses have preferences about the media by which they best learn. Some like written messages (readers), some like oral messages (listeners), some react better to formal settings (meeting managers), some to impromptu conversations (corridor managers). There are some who require a combination: multiple media managers, you might say. There are some who will let the situation dictate the chosen style or media. The point is, you must know your boss's media choice or most comfortable style and appropriately use it. You'll be more successful. Very often bosses have clear but uncommunicated preferences. And preferences vary greatly from boss to boss and over time.

THE LOCATION

Communication is often impacted by the surroundings, more so than we generally acknowledge in ordinary business activities. Often things are done in meetings that would be best covered privately. Choosing your office, a neutral office, or the boss's office shouldn't be an accidental occurrence. Sometimes the lunch counter, or traveling to and fro, works well. And again, a customized set or combination of these "location" choices might be best.

THE SEQUENCE ("30-3-30-3")

Consider whether a brief or casual presentation should occur first. Then a more formal, complete coverage. Or the reverse. Many bosses enjoy being warmed up at a pace they can handle. Some like immediate full immersion. I have found it very effective to have prepared a "30-second" articulation (passing in the corridor), a "3-minute" presentation (part of a conversation), and a "30-minute" discourse (a presentation) and then a half-day or 3-hour agenda. Then use one or the other as the opportunity arises. Invariably all get used, but in the sequence, and at the time, chosen by the boss. And the preparation of these four "pitches" always provide its own value to my understanding and comfort with the topic.

QUICK AND BRIEF

Keying off the just mentioned "30-3-30-3" technique, I always found bosses tended to favor conciseness. At some point they may require the full research with appendices and questions and answers, but usually the hook which got their attention was one slide or a single page memo or a clipped, succinct answer to their question. It was like a proof that the idea was worthy. It could be reduced to simplicity.

TIMING

It took me years to understand that timing can equal, even surpass, in importance, content, format, and style. Timing might be the most critical element of managing upward. I thought if a conversation should be had, have it. If it's on your list to do next, do it. Then I began to see that some people were better in the morning, some were unapproachable just before they gave a presentation themselves, some were like different personalities when their own bosses were present, some were at their finest just before vacation or on Friday or after a successful board meeting, etc. The actual time during a day, a particular moment within a meeting agenda, or any day depending on what happened the previous day, was capable of swamping, either positively or negatively, my whole idea/proposal. The timing was more crucial to get right than what I had to say or how I said it!

THEIR TIME

Almost every manager is under continual time pressure, often being double and triple scheduled. In fact, it's thought to be (erroneously, I believe) a badge of distinction to be fully booked all the time. So bosses are sensitive to how well their time gets used. Don't keep them waiting. Don't use their time if it isn't clearly warranted. Don't make them regret their choice of how to allocate their precious calendar. And, most important, make it clear you're aware of their time demands. They need to know that you know. Then they'll be more cooperative with your requests for time.

DON'T TRY TO CHANGE THEM

Drucker is very insightful on this point (see reference). For many years I believed it was part of my job to reach, correct, and grow the managers above me. It doesn't work. They can learn/grow, of course, but on their own initiative. My energies to "fix" or speed up the process didn't take. In fact, it probably created more problems. The point is to take them for what they are, harness their strengths, play to their motivations. Save your time and energy for that. Direct "change agenting" upwards is often dysfunctional and sometimes destructive to a relationship. Use your boss as a resource in whatever way the resource can be put into play.

THEY WILL DO WHAT MAKES THEM LOOK GOOD!

Sounds cynical. Sounds like managers only manage for themselves. But that perspective is useful in situations where you are presenting a proposal or looking for support. People's sense about what will enhance their own objectives or image is perhaps one of the most reliable foundations for support that's available. Learn what people would choose on their own if your logic or proposed value was taken away. What, fundamentally speaking, drives them? Then find a way to harness that. Besides, they'll often do what will make them look good regardless of your perspective, so you might as well utilize the forces that compel them. Even if you don't agree with them, it's imperative to know a boss's personal critical success factors (i.e., what MUST get done or go right).

"JUST NOTICEABLE DIFFERENCES"

"No surprises" is a cliche in management lore. Actually it applies to communication in any relationship. But how does one decide at what level a surprise begins? The way to do this is to understand that everyone has built-in boundaries beyond which something catches their attention, i.e., just noticeable differences. Maybe it's 10% over budget in any line item, maybe it's the top three in any ranking, maybe it's any negative number. Find out where the boss perks up or starts paying attention to any calibrated measurement. It is often personal, often different from organizational standards. Your approach must reflect that level where noticing begins.

"DAY-TO-DAY QUIET"

It's hard to get focused on a plan or idea when some urgency is shouting for attention. And often day-to-day matters are mishandled to a point where crises crowd out any possibility for reflective or considered longer-term judgments. That may be annoying, it may even be unjustified, but it's better to wait until the crisis is over. For better or worse, the short term dominates. A boss's agenda needs to be reasonably clear of the magnetic attraction of here-and-now problems to adequately free up the energies and attention required by your focuses. It is true that there will always be short-term urgencies, but wait for a time when they are reduced, relatively speaking.

OUTSIDERS

Bosses sometimes carefully consider information from selective sources outside their internal organization structure, e.g., club members, board of directors affiliates, trade association co-workers. So influence via those channels can be very effectively engineered; that is, convince the subordinates of a member of your board, or sell first the members of a trade association committee your boss is on. Such outside support may not be absolutely necessary to support any internal proposal, but at minimum it's a relevant checkpoint or testing ground that's useful to cultivate.

INSIDERS

Likewise, there may be positions, or perhaps networks, internally that can facilitate relating to a boss. Secretaries always are worth establishing a good rapport with, well before there is specific need. Administrative assistants fit into the same category for careful consideration. Some have more power to influence than is easily recognized. A boss's peer level will contain important allies/enemies to incorporate into any campaign of persuasion. Identify them early for possible communication or persuasive connection when such support is needed.

"LABELING"

Simply put, take a few seconds to describe succinctly any message or action to your boss. It may be obvious to all but the boss, or only to you. So labels like, "This is a rumor," "I don't need your help yet," "I think you need to know this," "I only want your early reaction," etc., help the boss know what is expected. That may not be the chosen reaction, but it helps a lot to pre-identify your desired reaction. There are already enough obtuse messages at the senior management levels in most enterprises. Make your message clear, with a label that communicates.

THEIR LANGUAGE/TRADE

Every boss came from somewhere once. Knowing that background and resultant lexicon, sculpting examples from that discipline, references to known truths in that profession, help speed understanding and facilitate questions or comments. Then using those questions or comments as a platform to build further dialogue or to adjust to another tack will further your process. Everyone likes being communicated with in their own special language, whether it's legal, accounting, sales, engineering, or whatever. It often only takes a little research or common sense to find out what that language is, or what the tools of that trade are, and then to incorporate them into your process of managing upward.

COMPETITION

A hook that almost always snares intended audiences is to explain, detail, sometimes even slightly exaggerate (usually not inappropriate because competitor knowledge is often late or sketchy) whoever is the prime competition in the trade of the audience. People seem mesmerized by whatever insights can be gained about those engaged in the same struggles, whether it be of one who is ahead, or perhaps used to be in the lead, or a past equal whose fortune has changed. Proposals are often sold for competitive reasons alone. Remember too, comparison need not be used only to promote similar actions. Opposite actions may be better chosen and are quite visible, viewed against the fabric of multiple competitors.

CROSS-INDUSTRY FIELD TRIPS

One of the most powerful learning frameworks is that of the "mostly unknown." Thus an unknown enterprise in an unfamiliar industry can provide a sort of intellectual jujitsu, harnessing your lack of knowledge in a positive way. Certain ideas, processes, or situations will stand out in higher relief, highlighted against your background of ignorance, and are therefore easier to perceive or understand in their simplicity. This is especially true and very quick in face-to-face circumstances. By visiting an unknown location, one can absorb a technical architecture, or a management style, or a certain personnel policy, in a flash (having less blockage by biases or experience) and then begin to think about applying it constructively at home. Of course, it is often difficult to convince bosses to visit such a site. Most feel more justified going to familiar surroundings where they "see" less.

REVIEW WHAT WILL BE DONE TO OTHERS

A good way to allow an audience to save face (not seem needy of education or explanation), yet not become involved, is to share a presentation which is to be given to others, especially subordinates. For example, an education program for middle management could be presented (only for information, of course) to executive management, who will invariably get quite involved critiquing and expanding. And in that process learn more than they would have allowed to happen if they were the direct audience. Likewise, parents often learn more helping with their children's school work, but they'd unlikely learn as much of the same material if it were presented for their own benefit. Receptivity is always enhanced by involvement, which is easier on someone else's behalf.

ACCOMPANY ON A LONG TRIP

Taxi cab rides, a long wait in an airport, a golf game, or multiple impromptu circumstances at some off-site location can all provide a platform of communications, a harmony of flow, that simply isn't available in the office. Interruptions are less imperious, usually are shared, and therefore are actually helpful to the dialogue. Many managers have told me they talked more effectively and at greater length with their bosses because of attending together a seminar in which I was involved than in months under usual scheduling conditions. It's worth setting up such an opportunity, even if seemingly inconvenient. I used to fly to New York City with my boss on the premise of other business there, "deadhead" back to Chicago alone, but having accomplished whole lists and wondrous pitches without being intrusive in his business day.

CUSTOMIZE/HOT BUTTONS

Whatever else can be said about senior executives, they invariably do not respond well to boilerplate or general-issue approaches. The references, timing, style, and content should be personalized for that individual, at that time, etc. A generalized model might serve well as the base for individualized whittling, but it should never show (i.e., a past date on a slide or an example useful at a different organizational level). Perhaps this could be considered too ego-oriented. So be it. Glide over somewhat the impact of ego, but never forget how important egos can be. A personalized approach is always preferable. Similarly, it helps to know what the current concerns or "itches" are, and to use those to enhance the attractiveness of a point or request. Whether or not managers are governed by the long term, they always respond to their own urgencies. So reach for them. Know and bend to the ever-present "hot buttons."

A "LIVING LIST"

Since most communication flows need to be refreshed continually, and the opportunity often occurs at a time when we're not quite prepared, it's smart to be continually prepared. "Have presentation, will start now," so to speak. A simple list of notes, always up to date, can facilitate small chances to communicate which open up — e.g., meeting in a corridor, getting settled in a meeting. And the continual updating habit will minimize your need for referencing or public retrieval of the list. The entries can just flow from memory into the conversation at hand. It's the Boy Scout motto applied to corporate executive communication. Carry the list in your date book so it's always ready for a quick "sneak" glance. This habit can also reduce the need for formal updating sessions with your boss, which are often hard to establish consistently.

SCHEDULE MANAGEMENT (COMMANDO STYLE)

Schedules themselves are a huge impediment to communication and understanding. No one has enough time or a schedule flexible enough to accommodate the incessant changes inflicted upon all levels, bosses and subordinates alike. So some guerilla warfare tactics may help. Drive your boss to a meeting, or meet the plane, or use time in the elevator or outside the door as a meeting breaks up. Obviously, many topics aren't appropriate for this "opportunistic" approach, but many can fit and that's better than nothing or a long delay. So be alert to breaks in "meetings-in-progress." Utilize the walk back to the office. Give the boss something brief and simple to read in a meeting where full attention isn't required. There are many "broken pieces" of your boss's schedule that can be salvaged. And the effort will be appreciated.

FORMAL PRESENTATIONS

Formal presentations are always important, often more than they should be. So one must become an expert. That's a whole topic in itself, but suffice it here to make a few suggestions.

- Learn to accommodate well to interruptions. They're often used to test your knowledge or confidence.
- Be so well prepared it can be casual, even "natural." The most effective points in a presentation are often made as an aside, seemingly, not as part of the main point of the moment.
- Prepare far beyond what's needed. Getting you off the topic is another test/stress tactic practiced by management. If you can handle it well, then return to your points — you'll have more impact.
- Be ready to risk. You're at risk anyway, so acknowledge it and reach for it. I believe presentations are for that purpose (i.e., to take a risk).
- Remember the "30-3-30-3" idea. Remember to pick the right media and all the other suggestions above.

CREDIBILITY

Good communication requires credibility of the person expressing the message. Improved communication absolutely involves increased credibility, better trust, or enhanced rapport. Credibility isn't just a descriptive element. It can be managed, like a project, with a resultant increase that shows up in better communication. Again, this is a topic suited for separate coverage, but the following is a starter kit:

- Presence helps, remoteness detracts, so be visible and visit often with those with whom you need credibility.
- As a first step, confidence in oneself is essential.
- Listening helps establish credibility. Commitment helps more. Results are the best support for enhancing credibility.
- Be early with bad news inside the channels. Be slower, both inside and outside the channels, with good news.
- Don't be wrong or careless in your area of expertise.
- Advance all arguments or alternatives, then follow them with a chosen recommendations. Don't just present your answer or choice. Other views must be adequately covered.

"SKIP-LEVEL" MANAGEMENT

While used for personnel evaluation for potential advancement, skip-level management can be dangerous for communication with a boss, depending on the structure and personalities involved. But you should know your boss's boss quite well. And give soft evidence of that awareness. The view from "far" above can enrich the view from below with surprising clarity, so be in touch with, and closely aware of, your management several levels up.

QUICK KILLS

Sometimes a fast result, without a lot of overhead, hoopla, or cost, can work wonders for a boss-subordinate relationship. Sometimes it's worth investing "extra," e.g., off-line, hours or unfunded resources borrowed from other efforts. This technique isn't recommended for ongoing transactions but rather for occasional ones, and often is very valuable early in a relationship, helping to provide a good "first impression."

BUILD THE PROPER CASE

Perhaps this just means do your homework well, considering all the above. All bosses respond well to "good staff work" from below. It just takes energy and insight to keep it going.

****

This list of 26 suggestions should help the student of managing up. These suggestions are not just to be learned once, but to be practiced, dwelled upon, and refined over the entire time of management learning (that is to say, forever). I have learned each many times over, and still need to remind myself. The argument can be easily made that there are no "complete" managers. There are only people who are trying to learn management, or people who think they have learned it and have stopped. No one is really finished yet. We're all students of the art. We are all still learning.

BIBLIOGRAPHY

Applied Management Newsletter, December 1984, National Association for Management, Wichita, Kansas.

Drucker, Peter F., "How to Manage Your Boss," *Wharton Management Review*, May, 1977.

Hegarty, Christopher and Philip Goldberg, *How to Manage Your Boss,* (New York: Ballantine Books.)

Jabarro, John J., and John P. Kotter, "Managing Your Boss," *Harvard Business Review*, January-February, 1980, Cambridge, Massachusetts.

Mezoff, Bob, "Boss Managing: Big Concern, Now Big Business," *Boston Business Journal*, November 4, 1985, Boston, Massachusetts.

ABOUT THE AUTHOR

Richard E. Dooley. *Directly responsible for all the Information Systems functions in two large corporations . . . consultant to a wide range of well-known companies here and abroad . . . teacher at several universities . . . a founding member and former President and Executive Director of the Society for Information Management.*

Dick Dooley spent 17 years at the First National Bank of Chicago in Retail Banking Operations, Planning, and Systems. For the last four years he was Vice President and Senior Information Systems Officer in charge of approximately 450 people in a leading IBM installation with a $15 million budget.

He was for three years both Senior Corporate Officer and President of a major subsidiary of Colonial Penn Group, Inc., involved at the strategic and the operational levels in an intense maturation period of that corporation, responsible for approximately 8,235 people in a large, advanced Honeywell site, with a $33 million budget.

Degreed in English and philosophy at Holy Cross, with an MBA from the University of Chicago, Dick graduated from the Stonier Graduate School of Banking at Rutgers and attended a number of technological and systems-oriented education sessions, as well as the Aspen Institute of Humanistic Studies, the Experience Compression Laboratory, and Outward Bound.

Since 1973 Dick Dooley has consulted widely in the United States and Europe, taught at Illinois Institute of Technology, the University of Minnesota, Northwestern University, and four of the leading graduate schools of banking (Rutgers, L.S.U., University of Wisconsin, Washington University). He has published articles and is a recognized speaker both here and abroad.

EVERYBODY WINS: THE THEORY W PROJECT MANAGER

Robert Lambert

Theory W is a strategy for software project management that provides a vehicle for satisfying customers and motivating employees by the successful construction of a product. The basic principle is "Make Everyone a Winner." By understanding the "win conditions" of the players, managing expectations, and actively searching out situations that satisfy as many win conditions as possible, the manager can create "win-win" situations where every participant's objectives are served.

The Theory W manager is a leader, a technologist who understands the product in technical and functional terms, an effective planner who can ensure that plans are executed, and above all a communicator who can detect dissatisfaction and convince participants that a new course of action is the optimal one.

Organizations can promote the development of a corps of effective project managers by implementing these measures: (1) define the position of project manager with the correct responsibilities and level of authority, (2) advance managers from the ranks of technicians, (3) train managers in the technology, the functional application, and interpersonal communications, and (4) evaluate managers on the quality of the product and long-term profitability, not short-term financial performance.

SOFTWARE PROJECT MANAGEMENT NEEDS A METHOD

Software projects are notorious for being late, over budget, and unsatisfactory to customers. "As many as 75% of all large systems could well be categorized as 'operating failures' [because they] either took so long to implement, cost so much more than originally planned, or are so functionally deficient that users are not reaping the expected benefits."[1] Several factors indicate that a better management strategy should improve the success of software projects:

- Chronic shortages of qualified personnel and the high turnover associated with a seller's market for skilled technicians.
- Widely varying levels of customer sophistication. In many cases, customers can neither describe the need in specific terms, envision a solution, nor anticipate the repercussions of alternative strategies.
- A generally accepted distinction between managers, with marketing and administration responsibilities, and technical staff. Often, managers do not fully understand the consequences of their decisions on the product.

Barry Boehm and Rony Ross have addressed the difficulties of software development by proposing a new management approach, called Theory W.[2] This paper will (1) describe Theory W, (2) provide a set of guidelines for the manager implementing Theory W as a leadership strategy, then (3) offer concrete proposals for organizations to improve software project performance by encouraging Theory W management.

THEORY W: MAKE EVERYONE A WINNER

The fundamental principle of Theory W is simple: "Make Everyone a Winner." The project manager's job is to identify the players, find out what their objectives are, and organize the project so that everyone's objectives are served.

Creating Win-Win Situations

Theory W's techniques for creating win-win situations among players with different objectives are taken from negotiation theory. Some of the highlights include:

- Understand how people want to win.
- Establish reasonable expectations.
- Match people's tasks to their win conditions:
  - search out win-win situations;
  - expand the range of options to create win-win situations.

Further, Boehm and Ross identify two secondary principles, expressed as follows:

- "Plan the flight and fly the plan."
- "Identify and Manage your Risks."

Planning and Execution

"Planning the flight" means developing a detailed description of project objectives, products, milestones, participants, responsibilities, approach, and resources. The plan "records the mutual commitment of the participants to a set of win-win conditions" and "provides a framework for detecting deviations from the win-win conditions." "Flying the plan" means adjusting it in the face of changing circumstances to actively maintain each participant's win conditions.

Risk Management

Boehm and Ross describe risk management in terms of risk identification, measurement, prioritization, planning risk strategies, executing risk strategies, and monitoring execution of risk strategies. They suggest a "flying the plan" strategy as the project progresses for periodic reassessment of risk, and review of the execution of corrective actions, with reformulation of strategies as necessary.

Theory W Is an Effective Model for Organizing Software Projects

Theory W gives managers a paradigm for running a software project. It is an effective approach to balancing the varying needs of technicians, customers, and the manager's superiors in the context of producing a system.

Furthermore, Theory W is a strategy for leadership in product development, not management of the process of developing the product. The production of high-quality products in technical disciplines requires orientation. The project manager must be a knowledgeable leader who can conceptualize the target system and mobilize all involved players in production of the system.

Managing by Theory W

First, it is clear that Theory W applies to a manager with responsibility for a single project staffed by about 10 people. A manager responsible for many projects or a larger staff cannot participate in team-building and resolution of technical issues to the level required by Theory W.

Theory W requires certain characteristics in this project leader. The Theory W project leader is:

- **A leader,** not only by designation as the manager of the project, but in the informal sense as the one generally acknowledged as the project authority and decision maker.
- **A product-oriented technologist** who understands the details of the system and its application, and subordinates the manager's role as administrator of the processes by which the project runs.
- **An effective planner and executor of plans,** with a well-formulated and flexible plan, a complete understanding of the motivations of each project participant, a clear mental picture of the completed product, and an ability to make decisions that change the course of the project and carry them out with confidence.

- **A communicator** who can quickly gauge changing satisfaction levels and convince participants that a new course of action optimizes achievement of all objectives.

The Manager as Leader

Theory W demands that the project manager be the *de facto* leader. Other management models have characterized the manager as an "autocrat (Theory X), a coach (Theory Y), or a facilitator (Theory Z)."[3] The Theory W manager is:

- A creator of product designs, schedules, and plans that enable creation of situations satisfying the objectives of all participants.
- A motivator who can persuade project participants to change their objectives and inspire them to work hard to achieve them.
- A catalyst of effective communications, ensuring the constant and complete distribution of information among participants.

These roles require a manager to have a high level of confidence among project participants. Regardless of the status conferred by position, the manager has to develop this confidence level by *earning* leadership status. "When the authority of the 'formal' and 'informal' hierarchies is in conflict, the ascribed status position of the formal structure is often second best."[4] To be effective in negotiating, setting goals, enforcing goal achievement, and imaginatively creating new win-win situations, the manager literally seizes the leadership of the project.

First, the manager acts like a leader: "being verbally active, demonstrating communicative skill, consistently initiating themes, seeking opinions and information, stating opinions and attempting to persuade others, and adopting an informed and objective argumentative stance."[5] Acting like a leader makes participants willing to find out if the manager can really assist in achieving their objectives. If their first problem is resolved, participants will seek the manager's assistance the next time. Successive resolution of more and more difficulties is how a manager builds a real leadership base. Beyond solving individual problems, the manager's ability to satisfy project objectives depends on his ability to solve problems by changing individual objectives in light of other participants' goals.

The manager must be as aggressive in maintaining leadership as in earning it. Challenges to the manager's informal leadership status can undermine his central role as a problem solver. Steady and strong support from superiors is required to avert these challenges. For instance, if the project would be better off without an uncooperative team member, the manager's superiors should provide a way for the individual to be replaced. If the manager cannot act quickly and decisively in such situations, project participants will not seek out the manager to solve problems.

The manager's role as informal leader is critical to the achievement of project goals. The manager is the only participant with the perspective needed to develop generally acceptable plans and solutions. If project participants resolve issues without the manager, then the solutions are likely to conflict with the objectives of those not involved. Without control over problem resolution, the manager cannot anticipate the effects of solutions. Then the plan begins to lose connection with reality, and the product diverges from the needs of the customer.

Developing the Product

The effective software manager understands the utility of the product and works to build the system users and customers need. Further, this manager understands the specifics of the technology well enough to conceive and build an internally high-quality system, one of the common "win conditions" for most analysts, designers, programmers, testers, and maintainers. All while satisfying superiors by meeting financial targets.

Building the Right Product

The manager has to understand users and customers and build the system they want. A "user" is one who will operate the system. A "customer" is one involved in approving resources for developing or implementing the system.

Business software projects generally have fundamental effects on customer organizations and the way they do business. To successfully integrate the new system into the customer organization, the manager directs analysts and designers in determining the needs of users and building a system to meet those needs, making sure there is effective and complete communication with users during requirements definition and later as requirements continue to evolve.

Further, the manager literally manages expectations of users and customers. First, the manager ensures that customers and users have a realistic view of the objectives that are achievable within the resources of the project. Beyond this, the manager also ensures that the customer takes the actions that only the customer organization can to make the project a success. For instance, the highest-quality reporting and tracking system can be useless if the customer does not appoint a system administrator. The manager should take special care to "make sure the right people in the client's organization have the right information about the project and know all the actions and decisions they must take to make a project successful."[6]

Building a Good Product

Often, "management" and "technical" project responsibilities are strictly divided. To develop a high quality system on schedule, there can be no boundary between the two. The manager who creates win conditions for designers, programmers, and maintainers understands the specific consequences of decisions on productivity.

New thinking about methodologies is surfacing in the ideas of practitioners like Fred Forman and Milton Hess, with the "Design First" strategy,[7] and John Palmer with "Essential Systems Design."[8] Both methods stress the need to develop and document a conceptual picture that encompasses all functional and technical issues early in the development process. Forman and Hess describe their strategy as an approach to the problems of "intellectual complexity, technical risk, and coordination"[9] in large software projects. The idea is to document a "system concept": a broad-brush definition of the system that provides a framework for the technical and functional detail designs. During development of the system-concept project, players "explore a variety of design approaches, evaluate them for feasibility, risks, schedule impacts, benefits, and costs, and select the design that offers the best chance of success."[10] The system concept permits group evaluation of technical as well as functional issues very early in the project, and provides a basis for continuing reevaluation of issues and refinement of the concept as the project progresses.

Refinement of the concept means more than simply adding more detail. The collision between abstract design and real complications can alter the conceptual design beyond recognition. Good software systems are like languages. A new language can seem so full of contradictions and exceptions to grammatical rules that it makes no sense at all. After study and practice, the student develops a "feel" for the language and begins to speak instinctively. Likewise, the collision between system concept and reality can result in a system that appears to have no underlying structure, when in fact its structure correctly reflects the complexity of the application.

The product-oriented manager controls the development of the design, recognizing the process of incorporating exception and complexity. This manager understands the consequences of each design modification, its effect on the original concept, and the trade-offs involved when the design is altered. The manager balances the need to retain the general structure of the concept against the seemingly chaotic tendencies imposed by the details of the requirements.

By being involved at this level, the manager can represent competing project objectives for the product. For example, he can balance the needs of users for inclusion of all the details, those of designers for an "aesthetically pleasing" design, and those of maintainers for a system that is easy to fix, and customers for minimum cost.

Lack of product orientation and poor understanding of technology is typical of American business and has been cited as a root cause of declining U.S. competitiveness in world markets. Gordon Bell calls U.S. manufacturing a "barren wasteland" because of the concentration on management of the processes of product development rather than the product itself.[11] According to David Lundstrom, "most large U.S. companies are headed by accountants and lawyers: people who wouldn't know an integrated circuit if it flew up their noses. The relative invisibility of engineers and a lack of respect for what [engineers] contribute to society are major reasons for the increasing dominance of Japanese companies in high-tech products."[12]

Proactive Planning and Execution

The Theory W manager understands the players, imagines new products, sets goals, creates plans, shapes expectations, and makes participants want to succeed. Planning is where the manager imagines a situation satisfactory to all participants, and develops a process by which project participants can work together to make the situation happen.

This manager literally lives in the future and in the minds of other project participants. The manager's first analysis when confronted with a problem is to envision a practical solution that takes into account each participant's interests. Then, the manager initiates review of the proposed solution among appropriate project participants. The manager modifies or reworks the solution based on review feedback, then works with involved players to implement the resulting course of action.

Effective application of this process of planning and execution requires that:

- There be a clearly formulated plan. (Project planning is not discussed in detail here since it is adequately covered in other sources).
- The manager understands the motivations of each player and plans partly for the purpose of maximum motivation of each participant.
- The manager has a clear mental conception of the completed system.
- The manager makes decisions in the face of incomplete information and enforces changes with confidence.

Maximizing Motivation

The first prerequisite for motivating project participants is simple: the manager has to believe in the value of the project and its ability to serve as a vehicle for satisfying the win conditions of all participants. This is the basis for the manager's energy and imagination in continual creation of new win-win situations.

Motivation is further advanced if each participant sees the manager as an advocate of the participant's own viewpoint. The manager walks a tightrope, acting as a proponent for each player's objectives while combining all objectives into a single win-win situation. This manager continually applies imagination in creating new options for conflict resolution. Successive creation of new win-win situations is an activity that builds on itself. Project players participate more and more in the negotiation process as they see its benefits in successfully resolving conflict.

Often, players who are assumed to have conflicting motivations are really after the same thing. For instance, Frederick Herzberg identifies production of results as the top motivating factor for employees, and lack of results as one of the top negative motivators.[13] This surely concurs with the objectives of the customer in need of a system, and of the project manager organizing the team to produce the system. The Theory W manager is diligent in searching out the true motivations and objectives of each participant.

The Conceptual Picture of the System

The manager needs a clear mental picture of the target product to develop and evaluate alternative strategies. Each strategy needs to be evaluated in terms of the effect on the product even before the objectives of the individual participants are considered. This is important for two reasons. First, the manager has to ground plans in technical reality for them to make sense. The steps required to produce a system are laid out in management texts, but Theory W goes beyond a cookbook approach. It takes technical depth and subtlety to customize a plan reflecting the specific objectives of the individuals involved in a particular project.

Second, technical depth is required for the manager to be credible as a project participant. A poor manager cannot hide the fact that he doesn't understand the details. This manager will quickly become irrelevant in design decisions, and will be unable to control events by leading the planning process.

Making Decisions and Making Them Happen

Making decisions with incomplete information to take actions that put the project at risk is the day-to-day work of the project manager. The Theory W manager has a framework for evaluating decisions: testing them against the interests of the participants. But the manager cannot share responsibility for creating courses of action and committing the project.

The effective manager seizes opportunities as soon as they are recognized, and executes actions to capitalize on opportunities with vigor and confidence. The alternative is to be driven by events and to lose the ability to protect the interests of project participants by controlling the progress of events. Machiavelli says it best: "irresolute republics never choose the right alternative unless they are driven to it, for their weakness does not allow them to arrive at a decision where there is any doubt; and, unless this doubt is removed by some compelling act of violence, they remain ever in suspense.[14]

Effective Communications

The success of the Theory W approach hinges on effective and constant communciations. Unless the manager is first a facilitator of communications, none of the other functions of the Theory W manager are possible.

As a negotiator, the Theory W manager understands the positions and interests of every project player. The manager promotes the creation of new win-win situations by educating participants in the positions and interests of other players. The goal is general understanding of all competing interests on the part of all participants.

As a creator of plans and design solutions that produce win-win situations, the manager is not only a technologist and designer, but a marketeer and persuader, whether selling new expectations to the customer or a better development approach to programmers.

As a goal setter and monitor of progress towards goals, the manager makes sure everyone has a stake in achievement of the plan. All participants understand the plan, its effect on their interests, and what it requires of them.

As an activist creating win-win situations in day-to-day project conflicts, the manager constantly talks to all players and registers their level of satisfaction with the project. When a problem arises, the manager creates a solution that is indeed a win-win situation by ensuring that all players understand how the solution advances their interests, and how it is the best possible solution for an imperfect world.

CULTIVATING BETTER PROJECT MANAGEMENT

To summarize, there are four general qualifications for the project manager: leadership, product orientation, effective planning and execution, and effective communications. These qualifications indicate specific actions an organization can take to develop, train, and motivate software project managers.

Define the Project Manager's Position Correctly

Theory W requires that the project manager be the individual with total responsibility for:

- Product design and development.
- Project planning, staffing, and scheduling.
- Contact with users and customers on project issues, including project scope, requirements definition, discussions of follow-on work, etc.
- Reporting technical, financial, and staff performance to superiors.

The manager needs sufficient authority to address project issues without a decision by a superior. Further, the manager should not be saddled with additional project responsibilities. Often a manager may double as, say, lead programmer. This has two dangers. First, the manager loses objectivity in balancing the conflicting objectives of participants. Second, the manager is usually overburdened and does justice to neither job. The successful manager has complete authority and responsibility for the project, and has sufficient staff to be a full-time manager.

Consider Software Managers Technicians

Effective software managers understand systems. They know how to program. They understand why structured programming is better, why inverted lists can mean fast access but slow update, which steps in analysis you can do without when things get tight, the difference between a good database design and a bad one for a given DBMS, etc. In conversation I have heard statements like this: "I'm not a systems person, but I understand the functional side." Saying that this person is qualified to manage a software project is like saying that living in a house is sufficient experience for construction management. Software development managers should be promoted from the ranks of technicians.

Train Managers in the Technology, the Application, and Communications

In addition to general management instruction, training for managers should focus in three areas: technical training in the specific tools used on the project, functional training in the business of the customer, and training to promote communications.

Given that the individual has a solid technical background, a manager can benefit greatly from in-depth instruction on the environment and tools to be used in producing the system. Training can improve the manager's understanding of performance and efficiency parameters, and can provide useful insights on the approach to design, coding, testing, and implementing the system.

The manager has to understand the business of the customer, the role of the user, and where the system fits into the customer organization. Training in the application business area would be necessary for a technically oriented manager to be able to speak the language of the customer. In most cases, this manager should also have the support of a senior-level analyst with subject-area knowledge.

Communication and leadership may seem intangible, but they have concrete parallels in business. Negotiation, diplomacy, and salesmanship are business skills for which training is readily available. Training in these areas will assist the manager in communicating with project players and creating win-win situations.

Provide the Right Incentives: Encourage Quality and Long-Term Performance

The level of product orientation among project leaders can be increased by treating profit as a constraint, not a motive. The continual maintenance of high short-term profits is a fundamental incentive in the U.S. economy. It begins with the financing of publicly held corporations in an atmosphere of speculation on the stock market, and trickles down to performance objectives for project managers that emphasize quarterly financial goals.

The project manager should be given financial targets not as objectives, but as boundaries within which to operate. Within financial operating constraints, the manager should be evaluated in terms of the quality of the product, its success for the customer, and the satisfaction of the project team. The number of software errors during integration test, the number of additional requirements identified after installation, and personnel turnover rates are examples of statistics that predict long-run profitability, and should be weighted at least as heavily as quarterly returns.

There is a crucial difference in emphasis between financial goals and financial constraints. Profit as an objective encourages an acquisitiveness that demands immediate financial performance, sometimes even to the point of addressing production problems by "simply importing the products instead."[15] Profit as constraint shifts the focus to the product, and encourages a manager to work within the resources available to the project to deliver a good system.

CONCLUSION

Theory W is a model for running a software project that results in a quality product while satisfying the differing needs of all participants. It requires special skills and abilities in the manager: leadership, product understanding, planning and execution, and communications.

Organizations that develop software can improve project management by working to develop a corps of qualified Theory W software project managers. Specific actions to work toward this objective include:

1. Define the project manager's role correctly, and support the manager with the required staff.
2. Advance managers from the ranks of technicians.
3. Train managers in the technology, the functional application, and interpersonal communications.
4. Introduce incentives that focus on quality and long-run financial performance.

Steady application of such measures to improve line management will promote project timeliness, profitability, satisfaction of requirements, and business competitiveness.

REFERENCES

1. Forman, Fred, and Milton Hess, "Form Precedes Function," *Computerworld,* September 5, 1988, p. 65.
2. Boehm, Barry W., and Rony Ross, "Theory-W Software Project Management: Principles and Examples," *IEEE Transactions on Software Engineering,* Vol. 15, No. 7 (July 1989), pp. 902–16.
3. Boehm and Ross, p. 904. Theories X and Y are compared by Douglas M. McGregor in "The Human Side of Enterprise" in *Readings in Managerial Psychology,* ed. by Harold J. Leavitt, Louis R. Pondy, and David M. Boje (3rd ed.; Chicago: The University of Chicago Press, 1980), p. 310. Theory Z is from S. W. Gellerman, *Motivation and Productivity* (New York: American Books, 1978).
4. Fisher, B. Aubrey, *Small Group Decision Making* (2nd ed.; New York: McGraw-Hill, 1980), p. 190.
5. Fisher, p. 226.
6. Rossotti, Charles O., "CLIENT MANAGEMENT: A Critical Function for Successful Projects" (Internal document of American Management Systems, August 23, 1989).
7. Forman and Hess, pp. 65-70.
8. Palmer, John, *Essential Systems Design* (Photocopied handout for a class delivered by Mr. Palmer for the Washington, D.C. Chapter of the Association for Computing Machinery, November, 1988). Mr. Palmer co-authored *Essential Systems Analysis* (Englewood Cliffs, N.J.: Prentice Hall, 1984) with Steve McMenamin.
9. Forman and Hess, p. 66.
10. Forman and Hess, p. 70.
11. Bell, C. Gordon, "The Fewer Engineers Per Project, the Better," *IEEE Spectrum,* Vol. 26, No. 2 (February 1989), p. 22.
12. Lundstrom, David, "Partnerships and a Professional Revival," *IEEE Spectrum,* Vol. 26, No. 10 (October 1989), p. 12.
13. Herzberg, Frederick, "One More Time: How do You Motivate Employees," *Harvard Business Review,* Vol. 65, No. 5 (September–October 1987), p. 122.
14. Machiavelli, Niccolo, *The Discourses,* trans. by Leslie J. Walker (New York: Penguin, 1978).
15. Bell, p. 22.

ABOUT THE AUTHOR

Robert Lambert *has 10 years' experience in software development and systems analysis, including extensive work with image processing and decision support systems. He is currently a project manager in the Systems Integration Division at American Management Systems, Inc.*

INTRODUCING NEW TECHNOLOGY THROUGH CHANGE MANAGEMENT: A HUMAN FACTORS APPROACH

Christopher Bond
Vincent J. DeFazio

Bringing new technology into the culture of an organization spells change; the principles of behavioral science tell us that change is unequivocally met by human resistance. And unless this resistance is acknowledged and managed using a human factors approach, chances are implementation will not be successful.

CHANGE IS A PROCESS, NOT AN EVENT

The biggest fear that end users have of new technology is not of the technology itself, but of the change that will occur in their jobs as a result. Paramount in the end user's minds are the questions:

- To what extent will my job be changed by the new system?
- Will my job, in fact, even continue to exist?

There is no doubt that jobs could be eliminated; in fact, much of the justification for new technology is based on a reduced head count. But what we see more often than the elimination of jobs is change in how jobs are performed. Technical change usually results in more control and greater accountability; however, it also poses a threat to the vested interest of the end-user in the status quo. New technology often exposes inefficiencies and those activities which do not add value. The challenge in bringing about change is to alleviate fear by convincing the target population that the technology will improve the way they do things.

The situation that emerges from introducing new technology will likely be characterized by jobs at a higher cognitive level, requiring more decision making, problem solving, and creative improvisation. Hopefully, the end result is a more productive, cost-effective operation, but it can be painful getting there. The Change Management Process, shown in Figure 1, is a way of minimizing the pain of change and ensuring that change has some permanence.

Most things are subject to change at some point. The first step in managing change is to *assess the situation* to determine if there is an existing problem, a potential problem, or a potential opportunity. The next step is to *make a decision* about what should be done to alleviate the problem or take advantage of the opportunity. Then it is important to *develop a plan* of how and when the decision should be implemented. The final step in the Change Management Process is to *implement the change*.

THE HUMAN FACTORS APPROACH

The human factors approach to change management requires a shift in gestalts, away from technician and toward facilitator of technological change. Human Factors is the study and development of design principles and objectives which focus on the human performance requirements of a system. It is an emerging discipline which is based on research in such areas as cognitive psychology, sociology, information sciences, and industrial engineering. While the systems

Figure 1. The change management process.

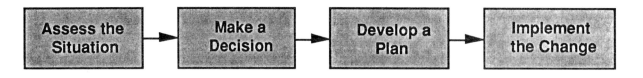

analyst seeks to ensure that a system is useful, the human factors analyst ensures that it is usable.

A human factors analyst can be referred to as a "culture broker." Culture broker is a term borrowed from anthropology; a culture broker is one who interacts to overcome communication barriers, such as language, values, and customs. Culture brokers in the information technology environment have a foot in each culture, and act as the liasons between the endusers and technicians. First and foremost, they are process, not goal-oriented. They are good listeners, empathetic, have a strong interest in people, and are good problem solvers. To the end user, they are advocates, ensuring a smooth transition into the future; to the systems analyst, they are essential team members, ensuring that the technology fits the business environment. Maintaining a relationship of trust on both sides can often be a delicate balancing act.

The operating premise of the human factors analyst includes:

- a view of change as a process, not an event
- the use of resources which optimize the relationships between people and technology
- a primary goal aimed at user satisfaction, not technical accuracy
- providing a service rather than a product
- a power base of human relation skills, not expertise in technology
- a vision of "people and technology in harmony"

BRINGING HUMAN FACTORS TO THE CHANGE MANAGEMENT PROCESS

The Change Management Process, as shown in Figure 2, is a helpful framework for introducing new technology; however, integrating a human factors approach is essential for a successful implementation. Without a human factors approach to implementing new systems, there is imminent risk of the new technology compromising the users, their tasks, and the environment. The worst-case scenario is when the end users revert to, or retain manual data-handling procedures. This type of behavior is a clear indication of "system failure." Other ill effects include degraded performance, frustration, loss of confidence, and the feeling of having been victimized. The diagram in Figure 2 illustrates how the Change Management Process provides a framework for the human factors approach to implementing new technology.

ASSESS THE SITUATION

During the Analysis Phase of development, the human factors analyst focuses on gathering data about the target population; this activity for assessing a situation is a means of understanding the circumstances under which the the users operate.

Our case study involves a major utility which established an information system for lowering costs related to vehicle inventory and maintenance. The intent of the system was to assist in the day-to-day maintenance of company vehicles and provide an information base for making management decisions.

The first step in assessing the situation involved the development of user profiles to identify characteristics such as skill levels, experience, and the constraints imposed by the work environment. User profiles are created through the use of structured interviews; they identify the perceptions of the different user groups, their motivations, how well they learn, their level of sophistication, and their biases. The scope of the profiles for the Vehicle Maintenance

Figure 2. The change management process.

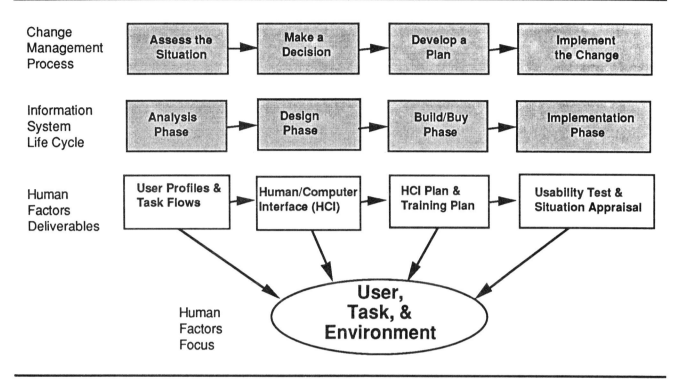

System included mechanics, administrative staff, and management. To provide a clearer focus for this article, we will discuss the Vehicle Maintenance System in regard to the mechanics and their immediate supervisors, the Chief Mechanics.

The user profiles established a baseline of information for the next step in assessing the situation, which is task analysis. Task analysis documents the existing work flow and provides a basis for determining the impact of the new technology on the user population. In many ways, task analysis is a way of discovering why a change is needed. Generally, change is necessary for:

- acting against an *existing problem*
- acting against a *potential problem*
- meeting an *objective*.

Task analysis identifies the way things are and is used for determining the way things ought to be. To the human factors analyst, the difference between these two states is an *existing problem*. Preliminary task analysis in the garages revealed duplicity of effort, redundancy of paperwork, and unreliable/inaccurate sources for the retention of data. The mechanics worked under high-pressure time constraints in a paper-driven environment.

Another important part of a situation appraisal is to assess *potential problems*. During a task analysis, the human factors analyst asks two basic questions: "What could go wrong? What can we do about it?" Identification of vulnerable areas in the user environment helped identify potential problems. Areas that suggested vulnerability included things that hadn't been done before, such as placing computer terminals in the garages. An important requirement was to have the terminals placed next to telephones since they would replace existing paper references such as 3 × 5 file cards. Tight deadlines suggested a strong need for usability in the system; the job of the mechanics is to fix vehicles or prevent them from breaking. They could not be expected to use a computer system with the skill of a data entry clerk. The system could not impose on their efforts. Their goal was to get in and out of the system by pressing the least amount of keys. The human factors analyst discovered that the Chief Mechanics ran their shops like independent entrepreneurs; this posed a potential problem because, sooner or later, agreement would have to be reached regarding how the new system would help each garage accomplish tasks. Additionally, it became clear that without the buy-in of the mechanics and Chief Mechanics, we might be faced with system failure; their use of the system (or lack of use) could potentially undermine the integrity of the maintenance and repair data.

A primary *objective* of the Vehicle Maintenance System was to track and automatically schedule inspections and preventive maintenance. The challenge to the human factors analyst was to persuade the mechanics in the garages that automating this process was essential to upper management and that if they chose to retain their manual methods they would defeat this objective. The key consulting skill employed by the human factors analyst was congruency, i.e., the ability to empathize and understand how change posed a threat to the endusers. The mechanics feared management would use the information system against them, e.g., by looking over their shoulders. So, by interviewing the endusers and assessing the situation, the human factors analyst helped alleviate some of the fears associated with the imminent change. The structured interviews and task analysis demonstrated to them that someone cared about who they are, what they do, and how change could best suit their needs. The results of this interaction were feelings of trust, confidence, and reassurance. Examining the current problems, potential problems, and objectives of the system made it possible to identify the *human factors* requirements of the system.

MAKE A DECISION

In the Design Phase of system development, the human factors analyst determines how the system will help the endusers do their jobs. The task analysis and user profiles developed in the previous phase helped define *why* a change was necessary. The next important step was to decide *what* changes should be made. New technology must fit the business, not vice versa; as a result, the decision component of the Change Management Process is perhaps the most important. Exploring the consequences of choice (alternatives of approach) is the key activity in this component of the process.

Two important techniques for discovering what type of change is appropriate to an environment are prototyping and storyboarding. Prototyping is a means of simulating a task. In order for prototyping to be most effective, the task must have a clear objective and a definitive set of operations to perform. For example, with a paper simulation of a screen, or better yet, an on-line simulation, a rich amount of data about the user's thought and behavior patterns can be observed. By carefully recording the user responses and comments, a human factors analyst can begin to model the system to meet the user needs, preferences, and tasks. Storyboarding is a similar technique which involves setting up scenarios which emulate the user's path through a given task. It is a powerful means of brainstorming to gather individual perspectives and, finally, of developing a group vision. Both prototyping and storyboarding are excellent tools for discovering the type of change that is needed; they are also a good means of identifying ineffective design choices early, thus saving the expense of retrofitting later. Another benefit of these techniques is that they help users gain a sense of ownership in the new system by allowing them to participate in design decisions.

In our case study, the human factors analyst set up meetings with the Chief Mechanics and performed a combination of prototyping and storyboarding. The scenarios involved visualizing how mechanics might use the new technology to perform their jobs. After gathering ideas about the environment and tasks of the mechanics, it was possible to begin preliminary screen design. The sponsor of the project had insisted that we consider purchasing a vendor package for the Vehicle Maintenance System; as a result, the human factors analyst rated packages with a 50% weighting in the area of flexibility. The reason for this was that, without flexibility in design, it would be impossible to tailor the system to the users, their tasks, and the environment.

The human factors analyst then worked with the vendor package and redesigned many of the screens which the Chief Mechanics initially found cluttered and confusing. The vendor, of course, was so immersed in the software technology that he felt the system was perfect the way it was. But there were several things about the system that needed to be changed in order for it to be usable to the mechanics; a prevalent example was the use of terminology such as *asset ID* and *domain* instead of vehicle number and garage. There was no reason to force the mechanics to waste their time making a mental translation from asset ID to vehicle number. The culture broker concept came into play at this point; as a culture broker, the human factors analyst knew enough about the flexibility of the package and the needs of the users to orchestrate an effective change. After being presented with the new screens, the Chief Mechanics, they felt reassured that their needs for the technology could be successfully met. By generating ideas and applying human factors principles of screen design, we were becoming more confident in how the new technology would be implemented.

The result of the human factors analyst's efforts in the decision component of the Change Management Process is a Human/Computer Interface architecture. This deliverable completely describes what changes are necessary, including screen designs, forms and reports, messages, instructions, prompts, on-line help, documentation, and training needs. For most systems, training is a key to a successful implementation. A good system design can reduce the amount of training, prevent errors from occurring, and improve recovery from errors which are made; however, the initial training is the point at which users learn the behaviors which are required for meeting system objectives. It is also the point at which many users first see the new technology and are the most impressionable. For these reasons, many of the negative impacts of the new technology can be buffered with effective training, which must be carefully planned.

DEVELOP A PLAN

Planning how and when change will be introduced is a complex undertaking. During the Build/Buy Phase of system development, the human factors analyst focuses on the acquisition and/or construction of system components based on the requirements and designs from the previous phases. Additionally, a strategy for implementing the Human/Computer Interface (HCI) architecture must be formulated. Both of these activities involve resolving issues, determining and scheduling tasks, and estimating resources and costs. The overall goal is to develop a plan for the change "to stick."

In developing a plan for implementing the Vehicle Maintenance System, it was important to provide the project sponsor with a cost estimate for tailoring the vendor package to each user group identified. The key focus was to extensively modify the screens, messages, and prompts for the mechanics (the administrative and management areas had already been exposed to computers and were much more motivated to use the system in everyday practice). With a go-ahead from the sponsor, the human factors analyst began working with the vendor to perform the necessary modifications to the system.

Another important human factors issue was to populate the database with actual data. The initial plan was to bring up the system with skeletal files and populate them gradually over time. This approach was risky because it would force the mechanics and Chief Mechanics to use their paper data-handling procedures in parallel with the system. The temptation to remain in the paper-driven environment would be too great, and the motivation to enter information into the new system would be overshadowed by the frustration of having to maintain two separate and distinct methods of record keeping. A plan was developed to place skilled data entry clerks on-site at the garages who would enter all the paper versions of the data. This way, the mechanics could witness *their* data being entered into *their* system. This approach allowed the removal of most paper versions of information in the garages, and encouraged the mechanics and Chief Mechanics to rely solely on the new technology.

Everyone on the project understood the importance and value of training, which made the planning effort much smoother than anticipated. As a result of tailoring the system to the users, their tasks, and their environment, the amount of required training was significantly reduced. The customized screens had an intuitive feel to them and included careful guidance and direction for each user population.

IMPLEMENT THE CHANGE

The final component of the Change Management Process involves testing and implementing the new technology, then evaluating the impact of the change. The result is an assessment of the new situation which leads us back into the Change Management Process.

Before bringing new technology into an environment, it is important to test it. Testing helps ensure that a change will accomplish its objectives without introducing a new set of problems. Tests should be structured to reveal known outcomes. Earlier, in the decision component of the Change Management Process, prototyping and storyboarding were used as a valuable means for determining some of the known outcomes. The designs which were developed through storyboarding and prototyping provided a basis for testing and for monitoring the effects of the change.

The role of the human factors analyst is to perform usability testing; this type of test determines if the human factors requirements of the system have been met. The criteria outlined in the plan for implementing the Human/Computer Interface architecture are a basis for identifying usability issues such as:

- user reactions
- speed of task performance
- frequency of errors and ability to recover from errors
- interpretation of information
- changes in cognitive demands on users
- subjective satisfaction
- retention over time

The objective of usability testing is to identify where the new technology fails to fit the business environment. A pronounced effect of poor usability is the violation of user expectations. If users have been involved in the design process, they will build expectations about how tasks will be performed with the system. When expectations are not met, there is a negative transfer (an interference of task performance based on previously learned patterns of behavior). Negative transfer requires an unlearning and relearning which produces unnecessary frustration. If the system meets user expectations, there is a positive transfer (a facilitation of task performance based on previously learned patterns of behavior). Conforming to user expectations is important, but their expectations can sometimes be violated, *provided* the new method is intuitive and makes sense to them. With user involvement with the design, there are very few "surprises" during implementation, and the new way of doing things will be met with a positive transfer.

With the Vehicle Maintenance System, a combination of alpha testing (in-house scenarios) and beta testing (on-site simulations) was used. The in-house scenarios helped identify fundamental issues such as speed of performance, error recovery, and ease of use. The on-site simulations illustrated how the system would perform in the actual environment. For example, it quickly became clear that pliable plastic covers were necessary to protect keyboards from grease and oil. Additionally, it was important to design devices for sliding the keyboard under the terminal to keep it out of the way of mechanics. These tests helped us bulletproof the technology before introducing it. Other techniques which made the tests successful were testing for extremes, incremental testing, stress testing, and retesting after making system modifications.

Once the system has been modified (based on test results) it can be implemented. During implementation, the Change Management Process repeats itself by presenting a new situation, calling for decisions to be made, plans to be developed, and subsequent changes. Monitoring this change process is essential for making the change stick. The bigger the change, the greater its impact, and the more formal the approach to monitoring it should be. Sometimes the monitoring effort will start out more intense and taper off when things appear to be going well. Often the expertise of those who initiated or implemented the change will be needed by those who are affected by the change. Additionally, some of the effects of the change will not be observed until a system has been in routine operation for several months. There is no formula for determining how long to monitor change, but most organizations tend to stop too soon.

There was a fear from the Vehicle Maintenance System users that once the change was implemented, they would be abandoned. In the past, they had witnessed that after a system was installed, there was no longer a commitment or the resources to support it.

The underlying concept of Change Management is that even though a change has been successfully implemented, a new set of circumstances will arise which must be evaluated. The monitoring of change, however long it takes, must be documented in the form of a Situation Appraisal. A Situation Appraisal provides an assessment of the new set of circumstances brought on by the change and determines if there are existing problems, potential problems, or potential opportunities. It also recommends decision alternatives about what should be done and a plan for doing it. What we see is a replay of the Change Management Process, except in the form of system support instead of system development.

After the Vehicle Maintenance System had been in routine operation for approximately three months, the human factors analyst put together a Situation Appraisal. This document described the impact of the change on the users, their tasks, and the environment, and provided strategic direction for supporting the system. The Situation Appraisal also became a useful reference for making trade-off decisions regarding system enhancements.

SUMMARY

Introducing change is a complex process, requiring an assessment, a decision, and a plan. Once a new change has been implemented, a new situation emerges which must be evaluated and acted upon. By using a human factors approach for introducing change, there is a much greater probability that the change will fit the business environment. And by involving the recipients in the decisions about what to change and how to go about it, the transition will be a much smoother one. As culture brokers, human factors analysts are a liason between the endusers and the technicians; their role is to bridge the gap between technology and the business. Each of the techniques of a human factors approach helps alleviate fears and generate feelings of trust and confidence. The results of this approach can be measured in terms of user satisfaction and are evidenced by a change that lasts.

ABOUT THE AUTHORS

Christopher Bond *is a human factors analyst at a northwestern utility. He has a certificate in the Human/Computer Interface, is a member of the Human Factors Society, and promotes usability in systems design as a guest speaker in local forums. As the lead analyst in his group, he develops guidelines and oversees human factors methods in system planning and development. He has worked closely with Vince DeFazio on various projects and helped co-author a life-cycle methodology which incorporates a human factors approach. He is currently working on a human/computer interface guide which describes techniques, models, and guidelines for screen designs and performance aides.*

Vincent J. DeFazio *is an innovator in the application and linkage of Information Technology to business planning and control . . . a visionary and implementor of business systems plans . . . a project manager and mentor who blends seasoned business knowledge and consulting skills with the tools of information technology to bring visions to ground for delivery of projects on time and within budget.*

Vincent spent 13 years in operations, staff, and management positions with major forest products companies, including U.S. Plywood, Champion International, and Georgia Pacific. He has experience in several disciplines, including business planning; engineering; construction management; financial, tax, and cost accounting; and computer system development. His ability to blend these disciplines has enabled him to deliver business plans linked to information technology for the utilization of timber resources from the forest to the market.

His entrepreneurial endeavors include proprietor of Managerial Accounting Services; President of Atlantis Construction Company; and management consultant.

Public sector and service industry endeavors as an information management consultant include: the development of Information Business Plans that link the strategic, tactical, and oeprational aspects of traditional business planning with state-of-the-art information systems for the State of Washington; project mentoring for the State of Oregon; architecture development, integrated systems project mentoring, postimplementation review, and content consulting for an application managers and developers guideline for a Northwest electrical utility.

Consulting accomplishments in applying technology to process planning and control in manufacturing and forest products include: JIT raw material procurement, log weight scale, and a variety of studies that identified opportunities to apply information technology for CIM.

Vincent holds a B.S. from The Ohio State University; an MBA from Jacksonville State University; and completed post-graduate work in energy and environmental science at Miami University, Ohio.

THE BASICS OF TOTAL QUALITY MANAGEMENT

Thomas H. Berry and Ferdinand J. Setaro

These two articles, "The Basics of Total Quality Management" and "Total Quality Management Applied in an Information Systems Environment," should be read in sequence. The former introduces the basic concepts of TQM to those who don't know TQM, and, for them as well as for those who already know TQM concepts, the "Basics" article illustrates the TQM philosophy of the company in the case study.

The "TQM Applied" article describes the successful installation of the total quality management process in an IS environment. Not only was this IS shop putting in TQM, they were converting or, as they prefer, "migrating," from a Honeywell shop to an IBM environment. These two mega-changes were accomplished in a synergistic manner. The article concludes with ten lessons the authors learned from this and other TQM installation experiences. They consider these lessons must reading before anyone attempts to initiate a total quality management process.

Simply stated, quality means meeting customers' needs, i.e., providing quality products, providing quality service, and having both the service and the product meet or even exceed the expectations of the customer.

Total Quality Management (TQM) is the process by which a company or division meets customer needs by organizing itself to engage in quality planning, quality control, and quality improvement. The process is led by top management, involves all employees, and, most importantly, is customer-focused.

The cost of not providing quality can be enormous. Most of the contributors to the costs of poor quality are hidden. Like an iceberg, most cost items (the costs of poor quality) are below the surface. They include such things as customer returns, lost business, rush delivery cost, excess inventory, and unnecessary field service. In the human aspect, they include such things as retraining, low morale, employee turnover, and lost time due to accidents.

The Juran Institute, which has collected and analyzed data on matters relating to quality for a number of years, says that quality improvement provides an enormous return on investment. Their figures show that the average management-level quality improvement project costs about $20,000 and returns $100,000 per year. A quality improvement project is a carefully planned, directed, disciplined, and well-supported effort to achieve a major, measurable, and permanent improvement in a product, in a service, and/or in a business process.

The Institute estimates that the cost of poor quality for a typical organization might be as much as 20 percent of sales and cites an interesting example. Consider a company with a current investment of $500 million, which provides $1 billion in sales and on which that company achieves a profit of $100 million. In order to increase profit to $200 million, the company would probably have to invest another $500 million in capital. However, using the 20 percent cost of poor quality estimate, if the company worked on improving profit through a TQM process, the Juran Institute says that 1,000 quality improvement projects (an investment of only $20 million) could also result in an increase in profit of $100 million. The Juran Institute concludes that quality improvement is not capital-intensive and that the return on the investment is among the highest available to companies.

Historically, most failures to make significant progress in quality are due to a poor choice of strategy on the part of company management. In order to make a wise choice in quality strategy, managers need to learn how to manage for quality. Then it takes several years to establish the habit of company-wide total quality management. Once established, a working TQM strategy represents a sizable competitive advantage for the long-term future.

Research shows that the most decisive factor in the race for quality leadership is the need of quality improvement. An evolutionary rate of quality improvement cannot compete with a revolutionary rate of quality improvement. Therefore, it behooves organizations to institute a large number of quality improvement projects and to keep pursuing quality improvement projects year after year.

A revolutionary rate of quality improvement requires a special organizational structure and a special managerial process. This structure and this process must be instituted by senior management. There is no delegating the quality improvement process. Senior managers show by action that they are prepared to carry out specific quality improvement projects themselves. They are the first to learn the concepts and techniques of TQM and the first to apply them successfully. They learn the language of TQM before asking others to embrace the quality approach. They become the steering body for the Total Quality Management process, a body usually called the Quality Council. The principal mission of the Quality Council is to approve the strategic quality goals, allocate resources, review project ideas, and provide recognition for work done.

The most important thing that members of the Council must do is learn to use quality tools and techniques so they can serve on quality project teams to show that they walk the way they talk.

There are two types of quality management. The first has to do with efficient productivity for quality improvement (doing things well), and the second has to do with effective productivity for quality improvement (doing the right things).

Effective productivity is achieved by improving the way quality is planned. This means that quality is planned into the process from the beginning rather than being added as an inspection at the end. It's the difference between avoiding problems and attacking them after they have arisen. The cost of fixing something after it has been broken is part of the cost of poor quality — a big part!

Achieving effective productivity through quality planning consists of identifying customers, determining their needs, developing product features that meet those needs, establishing product goals, developing a process to meet the product goals, and then proving that the process is capable of achieving its goals.

However, you have to start any major change effort where the people of the organization are, not where you wish they were. So before you get into effective productivity, i.e., quality planning, you must first achieve efficient productivity, i.e., quality improvement and quality control.

To achieve efficient productivity, senior managers first learn how to conduct the quality improvement process. They then choose what is to be improved and controlled and how to measure improvement. Senior managers establish those measurements as standards of performance. Having set standards of performance, they can measure actual performance against expected performance and then take action on the difference. The specific, universally recognized steps for quality improvement are:

1. Identify the specific projects for improvement.
2. Organize the project teams.
3. Discover the root causes of the problem through team analysis.
4. Develop the solutions to those problem root causes.
5. Prove the effectiveness of the solution.
6. Deal with cultural resistance to implementing the solution.
7. Implement the solution.
8. Establish controls and standardize the new process to hold whatever gains are made.

This process is led by the Quality Council, whose responsibilities are:

1. Establishing the quality framework
2. Developing the process for nominating, screening, and selecting projects
3. Developing a process for assigning teams to projects

4. Developing a way of selecting teams and providing the needed training
5. Structuring the process for making improvements

In developing the quality framework, the following resources must be provided:

1. Time for teams to pursue their projects
2. Facilitators (specially trained quality coaches or advisors)
3. Diagnostic support (data analysis expertise)
4. Training
5. Review process
6. Means for dissemination of information
7. Revision of the merit rating system
8. Revision of business planning

The first six above are part of the initial implementation. The last two are the revisions typically begun as a TQM process takes hold.

CONCLUSION

In conclusion, a successfully completed improvement project requires teamwork, statistical skills, definable data, and the discipline to avoid presuming root causes and solutions. Causes must be determined through careful, fact-based analysis. Hunches, guesses, and biases must be avoided at all costs. Also to be avoided is anyone who tells you TQM can be done PDQ.

ABOUT THE AUTHORS

Thomas H. Berry *is Quality Management Director for the Vanguard Group of Valley Forge, PA. Prior to joining Vanguard in 1990, Mr. Berry was Vice President, Quality Management and Corporate Training, for Colonial Penn Group, Inc., a subsidiary of FPL Group, Inc. (Florida Power & Light).*

He is a member of the Association of Internal Management Consultants, the Association for Quality and Participation, the American Society for Quality Control, and the Philadelphia Area Council for Excellence.

Mr. Berry is the author of Managing the Total Quality Transformation, *McGraw-Hill, which will be available in September 1990.*

Ferdie Setaro *is the Managing Director of TLE Consultants, a member of The Dooley Group. He also holds the position of Organization Development and Training Officer for The Vanguard Group of Investment Companies, one of the nation's fastest growing financial services organizations and the leading no-load mutual fund company.*

His IS consulting focuses on linking IS to the business and improving its organization, people, and total quality management. He has managed and taught, consulted and written about the non-technical aspects of DP and IS for over 25 years. His early works include "How to Use the Computer as a Management Tool," AMACOM, 1972, and "Auditing MIS," 1974.

He has more recently been published by the Center for Information Management Studies, the Association of Internal Management Consultants, and QED Information Sciences.

TOTAL QUALITY MANAGEMENT IN AN INFORMATION SYSTEMS ENVIRONMENT

Thomas H. Berry and Ferdinand J. Setaro

These two articles, "The Basics of Total Quality Management" and "Total Quality Management Applied in an Information Systems Environment," should be read in sequence. The former introduces the basic concepts of TQM to those who don't know TQM, and, for them as well as for those who already know TQM concepts, the "Basics" article illustrates the TQM philosophy of the company in the case study.

The "TQM Applied" article describes the successful installation of the total quality management process in an IS environment. Not only was this IS shop putting in TQM, they were converting or, as they prefer, "migrating," from a Honeywell shop to an IBM environment. These two mega-changes were accomplished in a synergistic manner. The article concludes with ten lessons the authors learned from this and other TQM installation experiences. They consider these lessons must reading before anyone attempts to initiate a total quality management process.

Some of the buzz words in American business today are "Total Quality Management," "Quality Deployment," "Continuous Improvement Process" and "*aiza*" (Japanese for continuous improvement.) All these terms refer to a style of management or a management process designed to improve quality and customer focus by involving teams or groups in a structured, fact-based problem-solving process.

In 1989, for the first time in history, a U.S. company won what is considered the highest award for quality management. "Quality is Job One" is the motto of the Ford Motor Company and "Quality" is now in almost every other corporate advertisement you see or hear.

However, as with most new technologies or emerging management techniques — even those with substance — the rhetoric often outstrips reality.

For example, there is a story about one of America's larger companies trumpeting in its advertisements its great concentration on quality as part of its company culture (another of today's management buzz words). The story goes that a quality task team brought a specific idea to top management and pointed out the potential important impact on the quality of the company's product if they were allowed to proceed to implementation. Top management responded with words like: "Tell us how many employees we can lay off because of this idea and then we'll tell you if you can do it."

Projects that look to reduce staff we call "cost cutting," and cost cutting rarely results in sustainable quality improvement. On the other hand, quality improvement projects very often result in cost cutting.

Needless to say, the quality improvement suggestion made at the above quality-trumpeting company was never implemented. That company still touts its "quality process."

All this is but prologue to raising the question: If total quality management is praised much more than practiced, can it be implemented successfully in an information systems environment? The answer is yes and is illustrated by one company that has done it.

© Copyright 1990 by Ferdinand Setaro and Thomas H. Berry

INTRODUCTION

When a company buys a very large software package and installs it as a vanilla application, the managers involved, in order to use the new system, must change the way they work. Since that is usually unpopular, what happens is that the "vanilla" package is modified to fit the old management style. This often negates the advantage of using packaged programs.

For most companies, installing a total quality management (TQM) process also requires a different way of working. To use another of today's managerial buzz phrases, it requires a paradigm shift, i.e., a shift away from today's pattern of thinking about how work gets done to a new pattern. In this case, a shift away from seeing problem identification and problem solving as a periodic fire-fighting process, to seeing them as part of a continuous improvement process using total employee involvement.

Depending on your company's current culture, this shift in paradigm could be the next logical step in a progression that was started some time back or it could be a 180-degree turnaround. Experience indicates that either requires concentration and almost total management focus. This is true in any environment, including an information systems environment.

And, speaking of IS environments, wouldn't it seem that the last thing you would want to do is make that change in your problem-solving management paradigm, i.e., install TQM, and at the same time make a technical paradigm change, for example, a $26 million migration from a Honeywell shop to an IBM shop? Who would want to do that? Why, Colonial Penn Group Information Systems, that's who.

This article will address how the technical change to a new vendor and the managerial change to a total quality management approach to problem solving were synergized to help CPG Information Systems make one plus one equal three.

TOTAL QUALITY MANAGEMENT AT COLONIAL PEN

Colonial Penn Group, Inc., the Philadelphia-based, billion dollar, multi-line insurer and financial services subsidiary of FPL Group (Florida Power and Light Company), began implementing a corporate-wide total quality management process in 1987.

At Colonial Penn, total quality management (TQM) is a structured approach to continuous improvement involving employees at all levels and in all functions. CPG defines quality as meeting the needs of customers. Customers include both the insurance policyholder — the paying customer — and the employees of the company who rely on fellow employees in order to complete their assigned tasks correctly and in a timely manner.

The backbone of Colonial Penn's TQM process consists of quality improvement (QI) teams, the members of which receive training in a proven problem-solving process. This training includes the use of various statistical process control tools such as Pareto analysis, cause-and-effect diagramming, and the like. A typical QI team consists of three to seven members who frequently represent a variety of corporate disciplines. A team, guided by its leader, chooses or is assigned to a quality problem and devotes the equivalent of an hour a week on company time until the problem is resolved.

Since the beginning of the implementation of its TQM process three years ago, QI teams at Colonial Penn have completed dozens of problem-solving projects. These quality improvement efforts have resulted in increased customer satisfaction and millions of dollars in cost savings. Today Colonial Penn has 150 quality improvement teams actively working to solve problems — to improve work processes, reduce errors and rework, speed delivery of products, etc.

Colonial Penn modeled its TQM process after that of its sister company, Florida Power and Light (FPL) of Miami, winner of the Deming Prize for quality improvement. This most prestigious quality award is bestowed annually by the Japanese Union of Scientists and Engineers. Until FPL earned it last year, it had never been won by a company outside of Japan. Ironically, the prize is named after American quality guru, W. Edwards Deming.

COLONIAL PENN'S IS DEPARTMENT EMBRACES QUALITY

Among the first to receive quality training and to serve on a QI team at Colonial Penn was Ronald C.

Glidden, Group Vice President and senior officer of the company's Information Services Division. In 1987, Mr. Glidden, along with the other five top managers at Colonial Penn, completed a quality improvement project that saved the company nearly a half million dollars!

This positive experience so piqued the interest of Mr. Glidden that he quickly introduced TQM into the IS Department. Today, with a complement of 400 IS employees, the department has 24 active QI teams — one for each sixteen people on the payroll.

The authors interviewed Mr. Glidden and Mr. Joseph Miserendino, a member of Glidden's staff (and another member of management trained in TQM) to closely examine how a total quality management process is helping an IS department meet the needs of customers. Here is what we found.

TQM AND IS — A NATURAL FIT

Glidden correctly sees a total quality management process — particularly the QI team's problem-solving part — as a logical, disciplined, fact-based, team-oriented, continuous improvement methodology and one that is results-focused. He contends (and we agree) that this fits hand-in-glove with the professional make-up for most IS employees. Consider the logic and discipline, for example, that is required for programming and the team orientation and results focus required to bring a major system on-line.

At Colonial Penn, members of the IS staff were exceptionally quick to see the value of the TQM process. For them, it was seen in part as an organizational endorsement for their current practices and their professional mind-set. Since TQM was not a totally new or foreign concept, it was welcomed and put rapidly to use in spite of an already demanding workload.

DEFINING QUALITY FOR THE IS DEPARTMENT

For Ron Glidden, quality also means doing things right the first time. He applies both internal and external focus to this definition.

Doing things right the first time internally provides for smooth operations within IS, avoiding rework, waste, unnecessary delay, and the frustration and added costs (i.e., the costs of poor quality) associated with off-target occurrences.

Externally, doing things right the first time will satisfy those who are the recipients of products developed and the service provided by the IS Department. Sad experience with installing systems that did what the client wanted, but not what he later discovered he needed, leads us to add the caveat that doing things right the first time will not earn a high score if we are doing the wrong things right the first time. Therefore, "It is vital," says Glidden, "that we have a clear understanding of what our clients need." So, a quality product or service is one that meets the expectations of the client or customer and one that is right the first time.

But just who is the client or customer? Glidden recognizes four categories of customers. First and most important are the ultimate paying customers — those who send in the premium payment for an insurance policy. It is important for all members of the IS department to understand how their work eventually affects the ultimate customer. This is the "bottom line" of quality.

The second category of customer comprises the clients or direct users of what the IS department produces, for example, the employees of Colonial Penn's Claims Department or the telemarketing staff.

Third are the people who work within the IS area. They are in a customer-provider relationship with one another and must identify and meet each other's needs before anything can get done right the first time.

Glidden sees the fourth category of customers as the vendors or suppliers who provide material, equipment, software and the like to the IS Department. He recognizes that no vendor or supplier can adequately meet the needs of his IS department unless the department's needs are clearly communicated. The subtle point here is that even if you are really the customer, treat your provider as a customer to better ensure that your own needs are met. Glidden provides exceptionally clear and complete information to vendors. In turn, he expects this information to be used only for its intended purpose and not, for example, as a means of making an unrelated sales pitch.

GETTING STARTED

Colonial Penn's IS Department launched their total quality management effort without hesitation. Glidden held a meeting of all 400 IS staff members to announce and explain TQM and asked each of the senior IS managers to identify a quality problem that could be investigated by a QI team. A sense of urgency was added when Glidden pointed out that "Those who don't identify a problem quickly may find all of the best ones soon spoken for." Problem ideas rolled in and Glidden selected the ones to be investigated.

Six problem areas were initially chosen and scheduled for solution. QI team leaders were designated and members chosen for the teams. With the teams formed, training was provided covering QI tools and techniques. Immediately upon completing training, the teams began meeting to pursue their projects.

Many of the QI projects chosen had impact outside the IS department, so some team members were recruited from such other Colonial Penn departments as Financial, Actuarial, Marketing, and Customer Service. The cross-functional approach is quite effective, since most quality problems have roots extending across organizational boundaries. By having people from a variety of corporate disciplines work together, you are not only more likely to find the best solutions, you can also improve interdepartmental cooperation and coordination.

GETTING RESULTS

Quality improvement projects come in a variety of sizes, from mega-sized, like "How do we solve world hunger?" to more manageable, mini-sized projects. Mini-sized projects are the type usually recommended by quality experts. They have found that it is easy to get bogged down or sidetracked and frustrated if too large a problem is chosen.

However, like most companies new to TQM, Colonial Penn and its IS Department did, at first, target some near-world-hunger-sized issues. Nonetheless, some impressive results were achieved. For example, in IS two projects related to batch overnight systems runtime were completed. In each, runtime was reduced by 30 to 50 percent! According to Ron Glidden, reduced system runtime is an extremely valuable improvement. At Colonial Penn, it means, for example, that the on-line systems are available for a longer period of time for Pacific time zone employees.

Another project resulted in reducing by 40 percent the time it takes to complete the corporation's monthly financial report — a significant accomplishment.

Micro-sized projects pay off, too. One IS quality team worked to reduce the time it takes to process travel and entertainment expense reimbursements for employees. They succeeded in reducing the processing cycle from 19 days to 4 to 6 days. Another team found that Colonial Penn was paying $12,000 per year in late charges related to the company's telephone bill. The team quickly brought this situation under control. Now late charges are virtually nonexistent. The employees involved in achieving these results felt quite proud of their accomplishments.

These smaller projects are invaluable as a way to allow junior or less experienced people to become involved in the process and also as a training ground in effective problem solving.

Sometimes in the TQM process, problems are uncovered other than those the team started to analyze. One IS team was investigating a health claims coverage issue. During the analysis phase, they discovered that under certain conditions, when customers did not pay their premium, the account still appeared to be active in the policy administration file. While this would be discovered and corrected if a claim was made on the account, it greatly distorted the picture from an MIS perspective. The Actuarial studies (which are a basis for P&L and marketing strategies) were based on inaccurate data related to policies in force and the true lapse (customer turnover) rate.

Mr. Glidden commented that it is because of this type of problem that he has not yet mounted a serious effort to pursue implementation of Decision Support Systems (DSS) and Executive Information Systems (EIS). "We must have sound, accurate administrative systems to be able to use DSS and EIS techniques effectively. All of the most sophisticated tools in the world will not help if we're still working in the GIGO (Garbage In — Garbage Out) mode."

One of his quality improvement thrusts is ensuring that these administrative systems are cleaned up.

TQM results can also be measured in non-numerical terms. Improvements in organizational effectiveness are common with a TQM process. For example, Glidden sees a definite positive contribution to the thought process and focus within his organization. Today, the focus and mind-set are aimed more at identifying and solving problems. And because the employees are involved with TQM, this activity is not viewed as reserved for management. It extends throughout the work force. Says Glidden, "We expect to solve problems, and everyone feels empowered to be directly involved."

There were two recent examples of how the QI thrust has permeated the Data Division. While packaging Auto Insurance Rate Quotes, one of the administrative assistants noticed multiple quotes for the same customers. She brought this to the attention of management, who discovered more than 25,000 duplicate pending accounts on the file. Fixing this problem saved over $45,000 in paper and postage alone.

In another case, while printing letters and riders to be sent to customers, a print operator noticed several spelling errors on the documents. He stopped the job, and the problem was fixed the next day. Because of this attention to quality, Colonial Penn avoided many calls and complaints from customers as well as potential problems with state regulatory agencies.

One side benefit derived from the TQM experience concerns the way meetings are conducted. QI teams are trained to start and end meetings on time, follow an agenda, produce minutes for each meeting, and get the most from each team member. This discipline carries over to regular business meetings, which adds to the organization's effectiveness.

PROBLEMS ENCOUNTERED IN IMPLEMENTING TQM

The authors asked Mr. Glidden to describe the three biggest problems he encountered in installing TQM within Colonial Penn's IS shop.

First, according to Glidden, "We failed to provide ourselves with the administrative support needed to help coordinate the forming of QI teams, arranging for the training of team members, developing periodic progress reports, etc. Secondly, Glidden continued, "we also failed to provide the TQM technical support which QI teams sorely need as, for the first time, they attempt to apply the skills they've learned through their QI team training. QI teams, particularly new teams, need careful coaching as they attempt to follow the QI problem-solving process the first time." Data collection and analysis using QI tools such as Pareto charts, cause-and-effect diagrams, flow charts, and the like can be a challenge for TQM rookies.

These first two problems were solved by appointing and training a TQM facilitator. The facilitator reports to the senior management TQM Steering Committee led by Ron Glidden and, after extensive and specialized training, serves as a coach or internal consultant to QI teams. A facilitator also helps coordinate the key administrative functions mentioned earlier. Today Colonial Penn's IS Shop has one full-time facilitator who is assisted by several part-time facilitators. All are recruited from inside the organization.

"Our third problem," added Glidden, "related to the facilitators themselves. At first, facilitators felt fully responsible for the QI projects their teams were pursuing. We need to have these TQM coaches realize that they are principally advisors. The team members are the ones responsible, and teams must feel the true ownership for their projects. Once we got these three problems under control, our TQM journey smoothed considerably," Glidden concluded.

TOP MANAGEMENT'S SUPPORT AND INVOLVEMENT

The authors observed, and Mr. Glidden agreed, that top management support and involvement in TQM is a most critical success factor. TQM represents a major culture change that usually has to be accomplished on top of an already busy schedule and deeply rooted habits. And remember, in Colonial Penn's case, a major migration from Honeywell to IBM was well under way! (See sidebar)

According to Glidden, "Top management support was not a problem. Colonial Penn's Chairman and CEO had also received TQM training and had served on a QI team. He also headed Colonial Penn's corporate Quality Council and still does. In addition, PPL Group, which began TQM in 1981 and won the Deming Prize in 1989, was certainly supportive of our efforts."

Mr. Glidden sees his personal role in TQM as an active one. He chairs the IS Quality Steering Committee and is personally involved in reviewing QI project ideas and selecting team members. Glidden and the members of his staff regularly visit QI teams to provide assistance and encouragement. They also serve on or lead QI teams themselves. In addition, Glidden employs the practice of MBWA — Management by Wandering Around. Every day during his travels around the IS shop, he is asking his people how their quality efforts are going. The employees of Colonial Penn IS know that Ron Glidden cares, and they know this not just by listening to what he says. They know by watching what he does!

LESSONS FOR AN INFORMATION SYSTEMS SHOP

From our interview and our experience, we have developed the following ten guidelines for initiating a TQM process in an IS shop.

1. The CIO must know what total quality management is and what it demands by way of change in the organization's management process.

    At Colonial Penn, the TQM process (called CTE, Commitment to Excellence) was already in progress, and CIO Ron Glidden had already taken part in a successful company-wide TQM project. He was trained in the process and had experienced its success. He was able to adapt the company model to his IS function. If your company does not have a TQM process, then you will have to learn TQM concepts and strategies before deciding to adopt one. There are many books[1] and seminars available, but they must be supplemented by tutoring from someone who has successfully installed a TQM process.

2. If you don't have top management support, think twice about even starting a total quality management process.

    Since TQM represents major, long-term culture change, it may not have the staying power or the thrust needed for escaping the gravitational pull of the company's existing culture without a passion for quality on the part of top management.

3. Gain acceptance of the need for good customer service and of the four levels of customer service.

    Good customer service is an idea whose time has come . . . again. For successful TQM implementation, good customer service must be accepted by all involved, and the four levels of customer service must be understood and accepted as well. Level one is the customers who pay, level two is company users of our services, level three is the internal providers we deal with within IS, and level four is vendors and suppliers.

4. The CIO has to have a vision and ensure firm direction to the TQM process.

    The first Henry Ford is supposed to have had a sign in his office that said, "If you really believe you can, or you really believe you can't, you're right." In management terms, this refers to what is called the Pygmalion Effect: people rise or sink to the level represented by what is expected of them.

    From the very start of Colonial Penn's migration from Honeywell to IBM, Ron Glidden told his people, "We are going to be the best." He instituted TQM to help make that happen, letting everybody know that was the reason. He then drove the TQM process from the top to ensure firm direction.[2]

5. TQM problem solving must be a data- (fact-) based logical process.

    If you identify a problem and know its solution, then that problem is not a candidate for a TQM problem-solving process. It is a management implementation candidate. Just go solve it. But when the mega-problem is "eliminate world

---

[1] Co-author Tom Berry's book on TQM will be available from McGraw-Hill in September 1990. The title is *Managing the Total Quality Transformation*.

[2] Another way for ensuring firm direction that has been successful is for the CIO to sell his or her top management team on the rewards of TQM and then let the team use a more participative process to provide the firm direction.

hunger" and you are not certain of the solution, you have to gather data and use a structured problem-solving process to identify related mini- and micro-sized projects. In the very gathering of the data to develop those projects, you will have already uncovered much of the data needed for the eventual problem solution. The data-focused, logical problem-solving approach to TQM is an advantage for its installation in an IS shop. Information systems work, to a large extent, requires the use of data and involves training in various disciplines in order to accomplish objectives. Therefore, the transition from data-driven and logical processes on the job to data-driven, logical problem-solving processes for quality improvement is not a long drive, it's a short putt.

6. If TQM is to be effective in the long run, it must become part of the way people regularly go about their work.

   Because the TQM problem-solving process is similar to the process IS uses to do its work doesn't mean that IS people can make a very quick change to using TQM. TQM requires a much more participative and collaborative way of working than many IS people are used to. Most IS shops are organized functionally to do a job and pass it on to the next function, or organized by product and focus on that one product rather than on the process. Under either model, the people are used to being managed in a hierarchical manner, and they tend to see themselves as isolated individual contributors. The exception to this rule is when you have successful project teamwork. There you have the best basis for total quality management project teams. However, even those teams must be extended to include everyone in the IS shop. Everyone has to be included because Total Quality Management is not something you do in addition to your work; TQM becomes the way you do your work.

7. Training in TQM concepts and specifically in the QI problem-solving process is vitally important to success.

   Don't skimp on training! Managers and non-managers alike must understand TQM, and all QI team members must receive thorough training in QI tools and techniques. QI problem-solving training includes such components as data collection, sampling, Pareto analysis, stratification, flow diagramming, cause-and-effect diagramming, the use of control charts, scatter diagrams, histograms, cost/benefit analysis, etc. Knowledge of these QI techniques and statistical tools permits QI teams to isolate the root causes of quality problems, to determine workable solutions, and to track the effectiveness of the solutions that are applied.

8. Make the commitment to utilize facilitators to insure a successful TQM process.

   Facilitators are quality coaches and advisors to QI teams. A good facilitator is well worth the investment. Inexperienced quality teams in particular will benefit greatly from the specialized coaching. Quality problems will be more quickly and efficiently solved, and teams will be better able to avoid some of the false starts and frustration that normally face TQM pioneers in the early stages. As employees become proficient in TQM, the need for facilitators decreases.

9. Involve customers in your efforts to identify and solve quality problems.

   Quality means meeting customers' needs, and customers include the ultimate, external (paying) customer, the users of the IS products, other employees of the IS shop, and your vendors or suppliers. Representatives from these customer groups should be included in your QI efforts where appropriate.

10. A TQM process is nurtured and sustained through communications and awareness activities and through celebration and recognition.

    All employees need to know what is happening with TQM and how well the process is performing. They need to know what their role is and what is expected of them. As results are achieved, the success must be celebrated, and those who have participated must be recognized. Eventually you need to make certain that your employee appraisal system recognizes and rewards the TQM efforts of your employees.

    Let us conclude this article with one final piece of advice. Installing a Total Quality Management process is installing a new technology — a management technology. It's not a handyman's special. You'll need experienced and expert advice. But as you can see from the Colonial Penn case study, the investment has great potential payback.

MIGRATION: THE BEST-LAID PLANS OF MICE AND MEN DO WORK SOMETIMES

In early 1987, Colonial Penn decided to migrate from a primarily Honeywell environment to a totally IBM environment. We referred to this effort as a "migration" rather than conversion, because we were changing everything: hardware and system software, the Application Portfolio, staff orientation, and the communications network. We were moving to a new place, not just remodeling the old one.

Actually, we were at this point a dual-vendor shop. There were three systems running on IBM equipment. In addition to the mainframes, there were 21 mini-computers in the corporation that were not integrated. There were 27 application systems running on the Honeywell mainframe, including some that were very old. Our communications network was a hodgepodge of cumbersome facilities, and there was very little IBM experience in the shop.

The two driving forces behind the migration were to eliminate the redundant costs and operational complexities inherent in the existing environment, and to build a sound technological platform for the future.

By mid-1987, we presented a strategy that said we would complete the migration to IBM by the end of 1989: a little less than three years. Most people, both those within CPG and other colleagues in the industry, said emphatically that it couldn't be done! We heard the horror stories about migrations that dragged on for years, severe budget overruns, etc. But we did it. By October 1989, the migration was complete — just about two and a half years after our commitment to proceed. Now people are asking us how we did it. How did we beat the odds?

The answer is, "We kept it simple." Careful consideration was given to how the work was organized and to the technical approach.

Rather than have everyone concerned about the magnitude and complexity of the migration, we divided the work into discrete, manageable projects. The managers of these projects were told to concentrate only on meeting their objectives and not to worry about impacts of all the other efforts.

The overall migration was managed by a full-time coordinator and a set of senior steering groups. The steering groups worked very closely with each team to ensure quick decisions and adjustments as needed.

The target technical environment was also kept simple. We decided to use simple file structures rather than try to implement a new DBMS environment while we were migrating. The on-line screen facilities emulated the Honeywell screen structures which avoided new design problems and kept our staff working in a familiar environment.

Most important, we did not mistakenly treat the migration as a purely technical effort. We pursued and achieved total corporate commitment and involvement. To overcome the skepticism and concerns, we had to have some early successes. Therefore, we elected first to move a few systems with a high probability of success. These were highly successful efforts and proved that teamwork produces success and success fosters teamwork. All functional business areas understood the level of the commitment we had to make and the sacrifices we would have to make to meet our mutual objective. They worked very closely with us by providing information and resources, minimizing system changes during migration, and working through any temporary business disruptions.

So that is the simple story of our success: corporate communication and commitment throughout the organization, good but flexible planning, keeping things simple by breaking a complex problem into manageable pieces and controlling change, and effective teamwork to ensure early successes that build confidence.

You can see that the parallel work of migration and Total Quality Management had the same basic process. Our macro-description of that process is: interdisciplinary groups working, together unselfishly, to achieve a mutual objective of improving the quality in the corporate process and in our working environment, in order to benefit our customers and improve our competitive posture. And we know the process works!

Joseph R. Miserendino
Director, Electronic Publishing Systems
Colonial Penn Group, Inc.

ABOUT THE AUTHOR

Robert Lambert *has 10 years' experience in software development and systems analysis, including extensive work with image processing and decision support systems. He is currently a project manager in the Systems Integration Division at American Management Systems, Inc.*

JUST WHAT GOOD IS AN INFORMATION SYSTEMS ARCHITECTURE ANYWAY?

John M. Blair
Ralph D. Loftin

Information architectures are an elusive and sometimes ephemeral concept to discuss. Then you try to sell the boss on planning and implementing an architecture. One chief executive forbids his staff to discuss information architectures. "It is something information systems people do to avoid real work and spend money."

For the past six years, we have been working with clients to put some substance in our discussions and have definitive outcomes from architecture planning. We think we are nearing the objective. What do you think? Just what good is an information systems architecture anyway?

For much of the past decade, several of us within THE DOOLEY GROUP have been talking about implementing, (or helping others to implement) an *Information Systems Architecture*. Sometimes we called it an Overall Technical Architecture.

As our courage increased and our experience in defining and using the terms grew, we started to list definitions. At one point we had a presentation slide that contained at least 20 working definitions of "Architecture."

With more personal experience and the growing experience of our sponsors and clients, the definition list shortened and the words used became more concise. Today we answer the question of "Just what is an informations systems architecture?" with words something like these:

> *An information systems architecture is the means through which the organization's business mission is supported by information systems and technology.*

A sound architecture will create and support a harmony between what the business does and the (information-related) means of doing it.

SO JUST WHAT GOOD IS IT?

The sound architecture allows the individuals working in the information systems organization to work shorter hours, be seen in the company of others of good character, and maintain lower blood pressure levels.

More importantly, the sound information systems architecture provides a platform from which the organization can use its information to improve its place in the market. Information and information systems should never be in the way of sound business strategy.

An Example

> *A company selling machine tools decided to provide sales incentives in the form of a contest among its sales representatives. The contest was intended to introduce several of the company's new product lines to new-name customers. To win, the sales representative would sell a large*

total volume, achieve a desired product mix, and sell a significant percentage of the product (in the correct mix) to new customers.

The contest was announced to the sales force in April. By June there was a noticeable shift in the product mix sold. The contest was to run through August with the winners announced in September. The winners would enjoy a significant cash bonus and an all-expense-paid trip. Several hundred sales representatives were competing for the prizes.

The contest was called off in July. Unlike the recent contest embarrassment for Kraft Foods where too many people were clear winners, in this case, the data was not available to decide if there were any winners. Every sales representative received a small cash bonus. It would have taken months of hand calculations to determine the winners according to the original formula.

The data architecture didn't allow easy identification of new models from old models or new customers from old customers. The applications architecture didn't allow changes to be made in less than six months and then only if the few analysts who understood the applications architecture were available.

The financial service companies compete on the basis of data and applications architecture every day. If my bank announces a combined balance, interest-bearing checking account and low-interest loan deal today, your bank better be able to announce the same thing (plus a little bit more) by Tuesday. And know if it is gaining any more market share by next Tuesday.

On the other hand, if the architecture is well constructed, fame and fortune may follow:

Several years ago a "Mom and Pop" operation started to make sandwiches for the local convenience market. These sandwiches were especially good when microwaved for a few minutes, and as word spread, the business grew.

Within a few years, the business had grown to where there were two salesmen and an office manager, who also ran their computer, in addition to a growing staff of sandwich makers and delivery people. The annual volume was approximately $4,000,000.

The senior salesman and the office manager were discussing the need to add another salesperson and wondering if the cost would be offset by added sales.

He also noted that training was especially unclear since some accounts were highly profitable (so it seemed) while others were not. He didn't quite know why and certainly didn't know how to advise someone new to the business.

Several days later the office manager shared a breakdown of profitability by sandwich type by customer with the sales manager. The sales manager showed the listing to several of his best clients. They changed their ordering patterns because of this information, sold more, wasted less, and profited more from sandwich sales. The poorest clients had an even more dramatic improvement in sales as a result of using this detailed analysis of what sold and what didn't. Adding profitability by sandwich, by customer, by day of the week, added another boost to margins for both the maker and seller of the sandwiches.

We heard the story from one of the early employees just as the company passed the $20,000,000 annual revenue level and was being bought out by a national firm.

The "architecture" that provided a significant boost to the value of this company's products was an off-the-shelf relational database and applications written by the very busy office manager in a fourth-generation language which came with the database.

The firm "fell" into the correct architecture due to an overworked office manager with a high level of street smarts. He didn't know exactly what to plan for, so he planned to be able to change and extend the computer systems very quickly and at very low cost.

IF IT IS SO GOOD, HOW DO I KNOW ONE WHEN I SEE IT?

Information architectures appear differently to different people.

We found that four (maybe five) levels are useful.

ENTERPRISE LEVEL
The Enterprise Level architecture looks a bit like an organization chart which only shows the vital functions performed by the organization. Figure 1 is an example taken from one of our recent architecture development engagements.

BUSINESS FACILITIES LEVEL
The Business Facilities level describes the processes performed by the business and the role each of the functions performs in support of the processes. Figure 2 shows a Process-Function matrix from the same example.

TECHNICAL FACILITIES LEVEL
The Technical Facilities are general types of technology which are suggested by the nature of the enterprise, its people, the values, the functions, and the processes. Six categories of Technical Facilities are generally considered: applications, data, end user, telecommunications, processors, and systems software. Figure 3 shows the Technical Facilities in a "platform" or set view for our example.

SPECIFICATIONS LEVEL
The Specifications level can be thought of as the specific technical facilities that are available for use when a particular part of the architecture is implemented. For example, if a high performance, graphically oriented, end-user workstation is indicated at the Technical Facilities level, the specification may describe a Macintosh IIcx or a PS/2 Model 70 with Presentation Manager.

Sometimes a fifth level is discussed. It is what is actually in place, the current configuration or inventory of equipment and software. We generally don't spend a lot of time discussing this level. Change is where the opportunity lies. Change is planned at the top three levels and is implemented at the fourth level. Figure 4 summarizes the definitions used throughout this approach.

The Enterprise Level is usually comfortable to discuss with senior executives and other business generalists. The Business Facilities or Process-Function matrix is usually comfortable with the specialists within each organization. The Technical Facilities and the Specifications are home territory for the information systems personnel. If the "trickle down" of key data from the Enterprise to the Technical Facilities level is handled well, a harmony of technical platforms and business purpose results.

THE CORRECT ENTERPRISE ARCHITECTURE

Choosing the correct enterprise is, as might be expected, the most important step in developing the correct architecture. The temptation is to use the organization chart; every box on the organization chart must be important enough to rate a "function" on the Enterprise diagram.

Unfortunately, this is another temptation to be avoided. It isn't even fun or easy (unlike other temptations). From our experience succumbing to this

Figure 1. Enterprise level.

MID-WEST MANUFACTURING CORPORATION
ENTERPRISE ARCHITECTURE
NORTH AMERICAN SALES & MARKETING

OTHER CORPORATE	MARKETING	CONTROLLER	SALES COMMON	SALES SPECIFIC	EXTERNAL
CORPORATE LEGAL	Manage Existing Products		Collect Competitive Information		SUPPLIERS
SERVICE - Inventory control - I.S. - Service Centers	Identify, Acquire & Market New Products	Issue Invoices & Credits	Conduct Customer Training	Maintain Customer Equipment Inventory	CUSTOMERS
COMPONENTS GROUP	Provide Field Sales Support	Monitor & Report Financial Performance	Report Sales Performance	Sell to Manufacturers	ADVERTISING AGENCIES
GENERAL PRODUCTS GROUP	Provide Technical Customer Assistance	Maintain Financial Records & Journals	Service Existing Customer Base	Sell to OEM's	CONSULTANTS
WORLD TRADE			Changeovers	Determine New Product Req'mts Confirm Product Specs	
CORPORATE CREDIT & COLLECTIONS			Encourage Product Line Extensions & Changeovers		SERVICE FIRMS

JUST WHAT GOOD IS AN INFORMATION SYSTEMS ARCHITECTURE ANYWAY? 91

Figure 2. Business facilities level.

MID-WEST MANUFACTURING CORPORATION
ENTERPRISE PROCESS/FUNCTION MATRIX
NORTH AMERICAN SALES & MARKETING

		1 Invoice/Credit Customer	2 Develop Fore-casting	3 Develop Strategies	4 Price Product	5 Develop Market Programs	6 Implement Market Programs	7 Add/Delete Part Numbers	8 Add A Product Line	9 Add A Customer	10 Publish Price List	11 Maintain Customer Data
SALES	H Collect Competitive Info		X									
	I Conduct Cust. Training						X			X		
COMMON	J Report Sales Performance											
	K Service Customer Base	X					X			X		X
	L Changeovers (Not Industrial)	X					X			X		
	M Product Line Ext. & Ch'overs (not indust.)						X			X		
SALES UNIQUE	N Maintain Customer Equip. List (HD Only)						X			X		X
	O New Product Req'mts & Specs (Ind. Only)		X									

Figure 3. Technical facilities level.

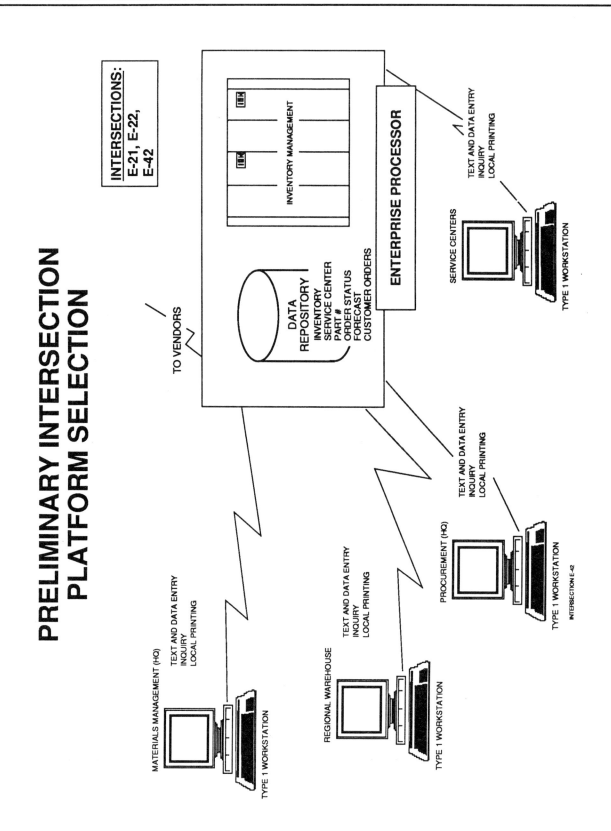

Figure 4. Information architecture business attribute glossary.

AUTONOMY: To what extent are individuals in the workgroup supervised as they perform the work? What latitude do they have in determining how the work is done?
COMPUTATIONAL: Work characterized by a high need for computational support. Examples are engineering design, chemical research, and mathematical modeling.
CYCLES: Does the volume of this work change according to day, week, month, etc.? Are there peaks or slow periods?
DSS/ANALYTICAL: Work involving the analysis of data utilizing standard analysis tools (for example, spreadsheets or statistical routines). This work may also utilize graphical formats for displaying results.
GRANULARITY: How soon must the results of this work be known or available elsewhere in the business?
INDIVIDUALITY: To what extent are the individuals who do this work able to determine how the work is done — how much independence do they have in conducting the work?
INPUT: Consider the information which must be available in order for the work to be conducted and for the intersection roles to be carried out.
INTERACTIONS: Indicate the nature and the timing of the interactions required among the staff, or between the staff and other workgroups, in order to conduct the work.
LITERACY: How comfortable are the individuals in dealing with information technology?
LOCATION DELIVERED: Indicate the business location where the work products are delivered.
LOCATION PRODUCED: Indicate the business location where the work products are created.
LOCATIONS: What are the business locations where the workgroup staff performs the work?
MEDIUM: Indicate the form in which the information is received: paper, fax, magnetic tape or disk, microfiche, film, voice, etc. Indicate the physical form taken by the work products. These may be expressed in terms of the business product (for example, butterfly valves) or information.
NAME: Describe the work products in business terms; for example, production forecasts, order records, customer service responses, etc.
NUMBER: How many individuals are involved in conducting the work?
ORIGIN: Indicate the business location and function from which the workgroup receives the information.
OUTPUT: Consider the work products created by the workgroup. These may be tangible articles or information for use by others.
SCHEDULE DELIVERED: Indicate the schedules on which the work products are delivered to those who receive them.
SCHEDULE PRODUCED: Indicate the schedules, if any, for the creation of the work products: ad-hoc, daily, weekly, etc.
SECURITY/PRIVACY: Indicate the extent to which this information must be safeguarded from disclosure outside the workgroup or the enterprise.
SHARING: Indicate the extent to which this same information must be available to others in the business.
STAFF: Consider the individuals who perform the work necessary to carry out the roles defined for the workgroup.
STRATEGIC VALUE: What is the strategic significance of the work? Is this work essential to a stated corporate strategy? Show as low, medium, high.
SUBJECTS: Indicate the general categories of information utilized in doing the work. For example, product, customer, sales, orders, competitor, etc. It is not necessary to show report names or other detail at this time.
TRANSACTIONAL: Work which is repetitive in nature; often undertaken in response to some event. The work may be simple (for example, data entry) or complex (for example, creating an order).
TYPE: Indicate whether the work product is informational or non-informational. If informational, indicate the type: text (alphanumeric); line drawings, charts or graphs (graphics); sketches or pictures (image); or video.
VALUE: Indicate whether this information would have intrinsic value as a product if sold separately. For example, demographic information obtained through marketing research efforts often has value to others in entirely different businesses who serve the same markets. Remember, here we are considering the free market value of the information, not the strategic value to the business.
VOLUME: A measure of workload in business terms. For example, if the work involves developing forecasts, how many forecasts are done per month/quarter/year; how many per product line, division, business unit, market, etc. Indicate the volume of information which must be handled in order to accomplish the work, using a "paper equivalent" method of measuring. For example, a paragraph, page or few pages, notebook, file drawer, file cabinet, etc.
WHERE USED: Indicate the business location where the information must be available.
WORK: Consider the activities necessary to carry out the intersection roles.

temptation and from running down other blind alleys, several guides have resulted.

There are usually only six (plus or minus two) key organizations in an enterprise.

Each organization usually has only four (plus or minus two) key functions.

Each enterprise usually has only nine (plus or minus three) mission critical processes.

In addition, the typical staff support groups do not show up in the Enterprise diagram, except through their support of the key line organizations. While consistent with the dictionary definition of staff (assistants to managers and executives), egos and ambition often cause this "omission" to be hotly contested. Support is received from Michael Porter's value chain analysis (see his books on strategic advantage and competitive advantage). In fact, the organizations which do show up on the Enterprise diagram are very similar to the links in Porter's value chain.

These few functions and processes are dramatically less (nearly an order of magnitude) than those defined within IBM's Business Systems Planning (BSP) guide. A typical BSP will address an organization (vs. a business enterprise) and will not distinguish between mission-critical processes and support processes. Between fifty and one hundred processes and a similar number of functions are developed and analyzed within a typical organization.

Good planning needs a correct focus. If the scope of the planning process is too large, the effort is unwieldy and often yields poor results because of conflicting objectives and strategies. To illustrate the risk, consider a fictitious (although not wholly) company, SGG, Inc., which produces plastic components.

ONE SMALL COMPANY, TWO VERY DIFFERENT ENTERPRISES

SGG, Inc. receives 70% of its revenue producing film containers for the major photographic film manufacturers. It has only four customers in this market, but produces millions of nearly identical film canisters. Because of camera industry standards, the only differentiation is the logo and color of the printed instructions on the canisters.

The other 30% of SGG, Inc.'s revenue comes from a new market, at least new to SGG, and discovered by accident: numismatics. Several of SGG's employees were coin collectors. Early in the life of SGG, these employees had obtained permission to buy small quantities of the canisters to store "rolls" of coins. They even had worked on their own time to make the correct sizes for various denominations and had changed the formulation so that the resulting containers were clear. Overall, the requirements for containers for photographic film and for long-term storage of precious metal coins were quite similar.

As an experiment, the coin-collecting employees took a small batch of their containers to a coin show and offered them for sale. They were sold out immediately and had orders for several thousand. Thus was born a robust new business for SGG.

The two businesses were dramatically different. The film canister business had only four customers, the lot sizes were measured in tens or hundreds of thousands, the margin was very thin, and the contracts were reviewed and revised annually.

The coin container business had hundreds (and growing) of customers. The typical order from a coin shop might be four dozen. Individual collectors had started to order directly from the company. The minimum order was held at ten pieces. Marketing through direct mail, magazine advertising, and coin show attendance was something new to SGG. The margins were great: sometimes as much as 90% before marketing and administrative expenses were considered.

From an information systems architecture point of view, there are clearly two enterprises to be considered at SGG. The film container business is essentially a commodity business. The information systems needs are inwardly directed, must handle build-to-order (large orders) manufacturing, and be very low cost.

The coin container business needs very good order management, very good response time, the ability to differentiate and track orders, and the ability to handle an order volume 1,000 times greater than the film container business. Coin container marketing needs to be able to handle relationships with advertisers, trade-show hosts, and numerous other outsiders. The product variety is growing, pressure is being felt to add single coin holders and other numismatic supplies, produce a catalog, provide outlets and products for Europe and Japan. . . .

A totally different information systems architecture is needed for each of SGG's businesses. The people serving the two enterprises are often the same, and there is little organizational recognition (i.e., department names or job titles) that SGG is in two dramatically different businesses. Yet if SGG attempted to serve both businesses with the same information systems, at least one (and more likely both) of the businesses would suffer.

ENTERPRISE EXAMPLES AND DIAGRAMMING APPROACH

A newspaper we worked with found it had three enterprises: Circulation, Production, and News/Advertising. A foods company spent several intense days deciding where its enterprises were focused around the market (institutional foods, large food chains, small independent grocers) or around the product (desserts, beverages, vegetables). A large manufacturing company decided it had six enterprises: two manufacturing, three distribution, and international operations.

One situation where the company was the enterprise was a small specialized education and publications concern. The decisions regarding what was key and what wasn't were much easier. Everyone employed by the company was on a single floor of an office building.

Sometimes it is necessary to consider the "corporate group" as an additional enterprise. Nobody likes to tell the bosses that they are not mission-critical or key to the success of the several enterprises in the company. The architecture analysis of the "corporate" enterprise may well reduce unnecessary information gathering and dissemination and focus on the truly mission-critical information.

When we first started to develop enterprise diagrams, we attempted to show by lines and arrows just how the key processes found their way through the enterprise. The result was a very busy chart without much value added. During analysis it is often useful to show the functions involved with just a single process. This may result in a dozen subsets of the enterprise diagram. These are much easier to understand and provide much better visibility into the "Why do we do it that way?" questions that should be asked about each process. Figure 5 shows such a set of enterprise diagrams.

BUSINESS FACILITIES

The way the work gets done defines the business facilities. Knowing the key processes and the key functions is the basis for defining the business facilities.

Early in the evolution of our analysis and planning technique, we would try to define, often pictorially, the way things happened within an enterprise. We would try to trace resource and information flow in business terms. The results often depicted file cabinets, telephone, forklift trucks, and the like. Another alternative was to show an expanded version of the enterprise diagram with the processes shown as arrows flowing through the functions. The graphics were interesting, but really didn't add to the intended goal of defining the correct set of technology to support a business.

We finally settled on a grid (matrix) with key functions on one side and mission critical processes on the other. We also clarified processes as being the evidence of value added by the enterprise *as seen by an outsider.* Shipping a product, taking an order,

Figure 5. Selected enterprise by process diagrams.

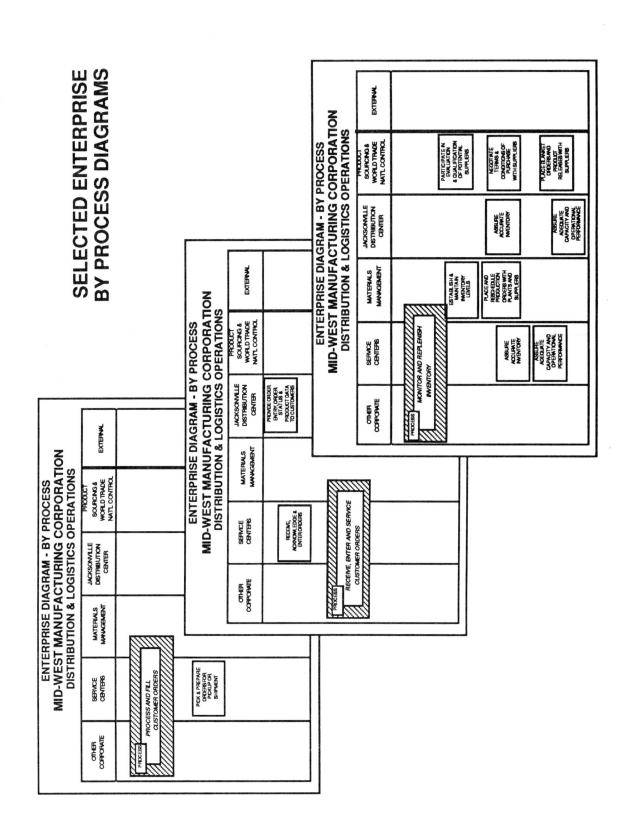

opening a new store were examples of mission critical processes.

Functions, key functions especially, are those actions taken by organizations needed to perform a mission critical process. The description of what this function does to support a process is called a role. Sometimes several roles are done by a function to support a process. Fewer are better. If more than two or three roles are developed, it is likely that the initial process description is actually trying to describe more than one mission-critical process. Or, sometimes, too many roles mean we really don't understand what the function does. Complex descriptions usually indicate low levels of understanding.

Figure 2 shows an example of a process-function grid or matrix.

SHAZAAAM!!! TECHNICAL FACILITIES FROM BUSINESS FACILITIES

Those of us who have been systems analysts or have hung around systems analysts are able to generally follow the process that a good systems analyst uses to select the right technical components for an information system.

The need for quick turnaround usually means a fast processor and lots of bandwidth in the network. High availability means redundancy, simple code in small modules, proven components, and proven developers. Highly sensitive data means sophisticated logical and physical security systems.

We also recognize some of the failures in the translation of business needs into technical form. Usually there are some traces of bigotry or zealotry present. Just as serious is a general lethargy which causes the analyst to be unaware of how new tools and techniques may fit a particular need.

Several distinct analyst types exist. There is the "small boy with a hammer" characteristic where all problems look like nails. One of our clients employed a very competent analyst who became infatuated with the PICK operating system. For some time, every request for service was a "perfect" fit for PICK.

Far more common are the analysts with the attitude that "It was good enough for my first program, it's good enough for this one." COBOL, an IBM mainframe, CICS, IMS, or a direct-connect 3190 terminal is a good solution for all problems known to man.

A recent twist is the geographic or organizational channeling. Come first to the PC support group with your problem, and soon you will see a PC solution for it. If, however, you first discuss your need with the standard applications development group leader, you will find a COBOL/mainframe solution to be just right. The organizational variant is that engineers do VAXs, Manufacturing does H-Ps, Finance does IBM, and the sales force uses Cross pens and bar napkins.

TECHNICAL FACILITIES FROM BUSINESS ATTRIBUTES

The better way to manage this synthesis of technology support for business need is to provide some way to enforce a higher level of objectivity, force a broader understanding of the requirements, and fit the solution to the way the organization wants and needs to work.

One way is to consider a broad set of the attributes of each of the intersections of the process-function matrix.

Attributes come in at least four types: work, input, deliverables, staff. A fifth attribute type which captures the values, principles, or culture of the organization can be handled separately or can be blended with the first four. In no sense should this aspect be left out of the analysis and synthesis.

Consider an example from our SGG company discussed above.

ATTRIBUTES OF A PROCESS — FUNCTION INTERSECTION

Suppose in the coin container enterprise there was a mission-critical process called "service customers and prospects." One of the functions of the marketing organizations is to "provide headquarters customer support." Most likely, the "service customers and prospects" process requires the "provide headquarters customer support" function to be successful. Let's look inside this intersection, and turn up the magnification on an imaginary microscope. Figure 6 may help illustrate the analysis.

The work done will be primarily driven by a customer or prospect making a telephone call or sending a letter. These come randomly and might total 20 per day. Each must be handled individually. The company has built its reputation in this new market through its very high quality product and knowledgeable, prompt service. Each of the individuals who take such calls has great freedom of action.

The individual servicing this intersection might have three roles: one would involve a customer who wishes to place an order, a second role might be a customer who has some sort of problem, and a third role would involve either a customer or a prospect who is seeking information.

The input to the person performing these roles is usually quite small in volume. If it comes by mail or fax, it is typically one or two pages. If the request comes by phone, the volume of data is the same. The origin of the input is anywhere the customer or prospect may be. The input is acted upon at headquarters.

The output of this job is also quite brief. It could be an order, a credit, or just information. It could be sent by mail, fax, voice over the telephone, or transferred electronically through the customer support workstation to the order entry or customer credit database.

The individuals who perform this work are typically acting on their own or with a very few others. Only two or three might do this work. They would have high autonomy and would have a moderate comfort level with information technology.

The values of the organization include high service levels, technically superior products, and low overhead. The company intends to be very profitable but believes that doing whatever it takes to achieve high customer satisfaction has been the reason for its continued growth and high profitability.

these tasks by first assuming a set of technical facilities and then "fiddling" with each to improve the fit to the whole of the attribute set.

First off, we have a multimedia situation: voice, alphanumeric data, facsimile, and paper. That suggests a microcomputer-based workstation and several telecommunication lines capable of handling voice, data, and fax. Paper gets messy quickly, so the addition of fax handling to the workstation will save paper and time. A scanner for the incoming paper will also do what the bankers call "truncation." The paper will be stored here; all communication out will be electronic or voice. Since existing customers call, and very rapid response is required, a customer file may be stored locally. Access to order processing and customer information is also needed. Depending upon how the rest of the analysis goes, these needs will suggest a LAN or a direct connect to the back-office computer.

Further refinement follows and as other intersections are analyzed, some compromises are made if the gains from standardization offset any loss in the match to the needs of the marketing support person.

Cost and technical resources also produce compromises. If your office is located in the middle of the San Joaquin Valley in California, service availability will further shift the final selection from the unconstrained selection.

The resultant set of technical facilities is often termed a "platform." On this platform are delivered the services needed by the enterprise at a particular intersection.

The alchemy is in the expertise which causes the transmutation of the base business needs into the right set of technical facilities which match the way the enterprise needs to operate.

So far we have not found a formula for this synthesis step. The most effective approach currently is for several knowledgeable, experienced, and low-ego people to work through each intersection. A room with thick walls helps.

ALCHEMY AND TRANSMUTATION

The systems analyst addressing this situation at SGG would likely start crafting the proper support for

SPECIFICATIONS

When it comes time to make, buy, or modify the "platform," the technical facilities need to be com-

Figure 6. The action is at the intersection.

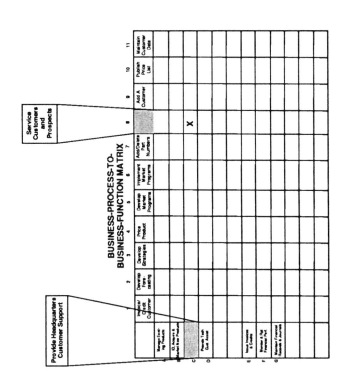

Figure 7. Under the microscope.

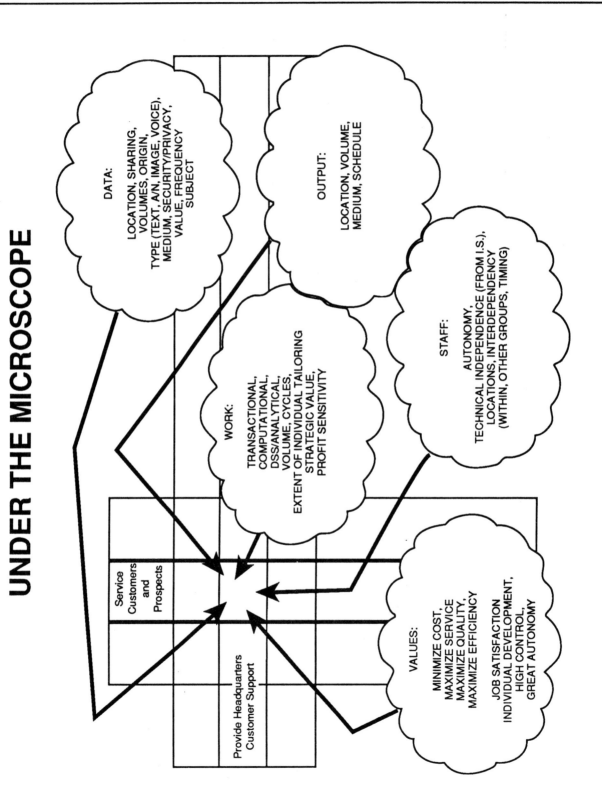

pared with available products and technologies. Compromises are always a part of this analysis because of price, support, talent, and timing. Out of the compromises come the specifications necessary to build or buy the required platform. The preparation of the specifications wait until it is time to act. We all become smarter with time and vendors are continually introducing new, better, lower cost or more flexible products and services.

STANDARDS

If an enterprise has 35 intersections of functions and processes, with 15 indicating the need for a medium performance personal workstation with communications, graphics, a relational database, and local printing, the need for a standard workstation has just been defined.

Similarly, if the corporate culture is one of buying and selling businesses, industry standard hardware, packaged application systems, and outsourced technical support are suggested standards. The business defines the technical facilities; the technical facilities suggest standards.

The architecture development process also suggests where deviation from standards is appropriate. The design engineer who likes to work at the family cabin in the mountains should be provided with two identical Macintoshes (one for the office, one for the cabin) because of personal preference, even though the standard is a PS/2. This engineer should also be encouraged to use a nonstandard communication link (Mac to ham radio to Mac to office LAN to back-office mainframe) because there is no telephone connection to the family cabin. The only condition is that the engineer continue to keep SGG six months ahead of their nearest competitor.

CAN THIS PROCESS BE PROCEDURALIZED OR AUTOMATED?

Partly.

The danger in excessive mechanization is that the procedure tends to take over and produce the results the procedure was designed to produce, not necessarily the results needed by the enterprise. The Business Systems Planning approach tends to produce an applications and data solution for all problems. It is the only output it can give.

Interviewing in order to understand what the right enterprises are should not be mechanized. Picking the key functions and the mission-critical processes are other areas which need the sloppy but highly sensitive touch of the human hand and mind.

Storing and handling the data gathered from interviews and analysis are great areas to be automated. So great, in fact, that we have done just that so we can concentrate on the message, not the media.

How about automating the transformation of business attributes to technical facilities? We think so.

If ever there was an application for a fairly elaborate expert system, it is this transformation. Today, we (along with our clients) are the experts. We can define most of the "rules" we use to infer that intersection 7C is best served by a shared database on a mainframe computer, whereas intersection 9D is best served by a standalone PC with word-processor software. Maybe by next year we'll have this all captured and smoothly automated.

BUT WHAT OF THE FUTURE?

Many parts of our society are justly criticized for solving last year's or the last generation's problems. The information technologists are in good company because they too tend to solve problems when the problems are well known and business has moved on to new and vaguely understood problems.

The future can be considered in the analysis at three places. Iteration and the consideration of multiple futures are the most effective approaches to dealing with what is yet to be.

The enterprise is a logical first step in thinking about the future. What about the current enterprise is likely to change because of trends, costs, technology (yes, it can come in here; consider what technology has done to the pioneer electronic mail service, Western Union), and the people running the enterprise?

The process-function matrix is another area to consider the impact of possible future scenarios. If the process-function matrix has a lot of "X's" in it, it may be that your enterprise is strangling in red tape and bureaucracy. Half of your authors believe that the ideal organization has one function responsible for each process.

As time-based competition and very high service levels are sought, the process-function matrix is a useful exhibit to analyze and question.

And the technical facilities are often sources for future state assumptions. If there was a $1,000 multimedia workstation with the power of a current 68040 processor with access to wide-band public communications, would that allow us to eliminate our credit and collections department? (Because we could do instant credit checks worldwide in the time it takes to write up the order.)

Thus the iteration. Would a new enterprise change the processes and functions? Would we change the processes and functions anyway? If we had a new technology and dirt-cheap prices, would the enterprise change? The processes change? The functions change?

AND AGAIN THE QUESTION, "JUST WHAT GOOD IS THIS ARCHITECTURE ANYWAY?"

Some wag said, "Businesses are optimally designed to produce the results that they do."

If your business produces products with borderline quality, the shipments are frequently late, the customer service surly, and the profit margins thin, your organization is optimally configured to do just that.

To change the results, the "design" of the business must be changed. If a design is to be changed, the existing design must be understood. It is what you are going to change, and unless you like to surprise your customers, employees, vendors, stockholders, and public, you had better understand how it now works and how any changes will change the way it works.

The process of developing an information architecture helps in understanding how the enterprises work. The way mission-critical processes are handled by the functions in the organization determines both response time (how long it takes to process and order)

and service image ("Yes, Mrs. Yount, your order was received on Tuesday, is now in box-pack-and-ship and will be sent via UPS this evening. The charges will be $879.23 plus your last month's balance of $234.76. We also show that in the last two years you have ordered higher quantities this time of year. If you plan to do that again this year, you will be eligible for an added 9% discount because of volume. Your payments can be spread evenly. . . .").

Quality products, quality service, and fast response to business transactions require a very simple business structure. Simplicity is determined by information flow more than product or material flow. In an increasing number of businesses, there is no product other than information. The information architecture is one way to understand and make positive changes to quality of the service and response time of your enterprise.

And you tend to buy the right computers, save the right data, develop the right applications, and not work as many weekends.

ABOUT THE AUTHORS

John M. Blair *has executive experience spanning both vendor and application aspects of information systems — product planning engineering, quality assurance, production, CAD, CAM, marketing, MIS . . . pioneer user of personal computers . . . university trustee . . . board member of several high-tech companies.*

John Blair has worked in the information systems field for more than 20 years. As Director of Information Resource Management for Honeywell's Large Information Systems Division, he managed an installation of over 60 mainframes and 100 minis. While Director of MIS for Synertek, Inc., John led the complete conversion of the information systems to a distributed processing environment spanning three continents, integrating systems components from dozens of vendors. He also implemented an administrative network of international scope which integrated personal computers, word processors, and data processing systems.

Recognizing in the mid-70's the power and potential of the microcomputer, John led a project that placed 200 automated process and test stations within Honeywell's large computer manufacturing plant by 1980. As a result of his own early use of a personal computer, he sponsored numerous pilot projects in office automation and professional work stations in the late 70's.

A graduate engineer from Purdue, John has done graduate work at Syracuse University, Florida Institute of Technology, and Arizona State University in Engineering and Business Administration.

An author and university teacher, John Blair helped develop an MBA option in Information Systems at Western International University, and now serves as a trustee and head of the planning committee for that university. John also serves on the boards of directors for several high-tech start-up companies.

Ralph D. Loftin *has spent more than 20 years in a variety of management positions with increasing responsibility in the areas of information systems and services . . . particular skills in strategic and tactical planning, organizational effectiveness, vendor relationships and contract management, operations performance, and capacity and resource management.*

As Vice President, Data Processing Services for Blue Cross and Blue Shield of Massachusetts, a $4 billion-health care services company, Ralph Loftin had complete Information Resource Management responsibility, including voice and data communications, reprographics and micrographics, mail operations, word processing and data processing, managing a staff of 700 and an annual budget of $35 million.

Previously, at General Electric's Information Services Division, he developed a programming service business for both government and commercial markets. He was responsible for marketing and sales, contract administration and project management and control.

For the same firm, Ralph also managed a contractor support group for a major NASA installation, furnishing programming, hardware engineering and equipment maintenance services.

He holds M.S. and B.S. degrees in Electrical Engineering from the Georgia Institute of Technology. Author of numerous papers and articles, he has spoken widely at national and international conferences. His work in the use of organizational effectiveness methods in managing the information systems function was the subject of a prize-winning paper in the 1982 Society for Information Management national competition.

Ralph Loftin serves on the National Executive Council for the Society of Information Management and was Chairperson of the Boston Chapter. He has taught at Georgia Tech, the University of Massachusetts, and Babson College, and is on the adjunct faculty at Suffolk University. He was appointed to the National Panel of Arbitrators in 1973.

WE JUST DON'T RESPECT REQUIREMENTS

Steven J. Andriole

We know how to develop a good, representative set of requirements for a computer project. We just don't like to do it.

Intense creativity is used to avoid talking to users (real users, that is), listening to users, convincing users that what we want to do anyway is in their best interests or that they really didn't need the computer assistance in the first place.

Now, the users of information systems are not without guilt. They change their minds. They find out something new after specs are signed and feel it is an unreasonable constraint not to be able to use newfound knowledge. They also let the computer experts con them into talking about projects in terms of computers vs. information needs.

Each new tool solves some problems but introduces new ways to avoid understanding what the requirements really are.

In 1988 the Pentagon spent about a billion dollars for 20,000 laptop microcomputers. Who did the requirements analysis? How was it done? How do you do a requirements analysis for hardware procurement without knowing what users will be doing on the hardware? Assuming that a long list of functions, tasks, and sub-tasks was compiled, how is it possible that a single system could fulfill all of the requirements on the list? The best way to select hardware, of course, is to determine software requirements first (and, of course, the best way to determine software requirements is to identify user requirements first). Given these design principles, how can we expect the 20,000 machines to be used optimally?

We do this sort of thing all of the time. We buy PCs for our homes the same way. Charlie has a Mac so I bought one. . . . Everyone has IBM PCs so I better get one of those. . . . But Brand X is a lot cheaper, so maybe I should. . . . What about the requirements? What are you going to use the machine for? What aren't you going to do with it? An enormous percentage of people buy PCs to do word processing. If that is the primary requirement, why do they need MAC IIs or PC 286s? Faster and more powerful is not always cost-effective. Magnavox and Smith Corona each have "personal" word processing systems that cost much less than $1,000. They do most everything that the other machines do, just cheaper, and because they were designed to perform word processing tasks almost exclusively, they often exceed the word processing capabilities of much larger (more powerful and more expensive) alternatives. If compatibility is important, there are low-end systems that support word processing, preserve compatibility, and cost less than $1,500. These systems can be upgraded if necessary and will run other-than-word-processing programs. If your requirements call for number crunching, then configure a system that crunches well; if you need color presentation graphics capabilities, then so configure your system. Criteria-based requirements analysis is the least we should do prior to purchasing a system — any system. The sad outcome of many investment decisions is dissatisfaction with the system, expensive retrofits, and often the complete abandonment of the initial system.

With big buys, the reasons why we repeat the "mistakes" are simple: money, money, and money. The reasoning goes something like this: if we buy many machines at one time and make the procurement competitive, we will encourage price slashing and thereby dramatically reduce unit costs. The logic, of course, is flawed and the economy very, very false. Unless the units can be used productively, they will become very, very expensive (regardless of unit dollar costs).

User and software requirements do not — unfortunately — drive large hardware procurements. In spite of rhetoric to the contrary, we really don't believe in requirements. We really don't believe in the tooth fairy, Santa Claus, or systems analysts. Even more unbelievable are people who do "task analyses," conduct "job analyses," or build requirements matrices comprised of user profiles, substantive tasks and sub-tasks, and organizational characteristics.

We don't really believe that elaborate front-end analyses pay large enough dividends. We remain unconvinced about the wisdom of allocating, say, 40% of the project budget to user requirements analysts. When all is said and done, we really don't like users very much (never mind what they think of us), we don't pay enough attention to requirements analysis methods, we go too fast, we don't prototype often or well enough, and we like to disregard the importance of "context," or the overall situational and organizational environment in which the system will operate.

The first important distinction is between user and software requirements. They are vastly different. Most of the requirements analyses conducted by systems analysts are oriented toward the specification of software functions and, by implication, routines. Far less effort is expended on behalf of end users, on the process by which user requirements are identified, refined, and validated.

The methods, tools, and techniques used to specify software requirements are very different from those available for user requirements analysts. We know a little about how to use software requirements methods, tools, and techniques (like the so-called structured techniques), but much less about how to leverage user requirements analysis methods. Unfortunately, there is more to be gained from the optimal use of user requirements analysis methods than the application of software requirements analysis methods. If user requirements are incomplete or ambiguous, then software requirements will be invalid.

This, of course, happens all the time. There are countless examples of elegant software specifications that bear no resemblance to what users actually need or want. Systems analysts are quick to flowchart software requirements, eager to draw visually pleasing bubble data-flow diagrams, and excited about playing with the new computer-aided software engineering (CASE) tools that help generate flowcharts and data-flow diagrams faster and more efficiently. (CASE tools are wonderful examples of devices that accelerate one aspect of a process while simultaneously undermining another. On another level, think of CASE tools as providing the opportunity to make great time, even if you're lost.)

This article deals with the front-end of the front-end of the systems design process. **It deals with the identification, definition, and validation of user requirements.** It also indicts the information systems analysis process for failing to treat user requirements analysis seriously. This article deals with problems. It presents some evidence that suggests that there are a number of problems that together threaten our ability to identify, refine, or validate user requirements. Since user requirements prime the overall requirements pump, if they are inaccurately defined, the prospects for successful systems design and development are virtually nonexistent.

WE REALLY DON'T LIKE USERS

Users are an unruly lot. They are notoriously inarticulate, uncooperative, and fickle. On Monday they tell us they want pull-down menus, but on Wednesday they prefer stationary ones. On Tuesday they want interactive graphic displays, but on Thursday they want alphanumeric tables. When asked to describe how they allocate resources, generate plans, or control inventories, they only provide the skimpiest details.

Users don't really understand how difficult it is to build systems. They don't appreciate all of the constraints in the process. They don't have any real sense of the complex trade-offs that must be made across, for example, random access memory and user interface software. All they really want is a system that helps them perform some complicated tasks.

How should blame be distributed? Given how easy it is (and historically has been) to bash users, another explanation is possible. It may be that users are inarticulate and inconsistent because we don't know how to work with them, because we have yet to refine the process by which we communicate with users. We may have problems with users simply because we have failed to develop the requisite skills.

Some years ago, a short but important book was published by Enid Mumford and Don Henshall that proposed *A Participative Approach to Computer Systems Design* (Mumford and Henshall, 1979). In 1988, Patricia J. Guinan published *Patterns of Excellence for IS Professionals* (Guinan, 1988), which analyzes the communication behavior between users and systems analysts. These books have several things in common. First, they recognize the importance of communication with users, but much more important, they underscore the need for users to become bona fide members of the systems design team.

Usually we see users as disjoint targets. They represent what we "have to do." They much more often represent constraints than design opportunities. We see users as roadblocks, obstacles to our success. The participatory approach to systems design requires user input, gives users design status, and makes them part of the iteration necessary to refine and validate user requirements.

Systems analysts see users as the indirect source of software requirements. Nearly all texts on requirements analysis start with software requirements; user requirements are treated as "givens." Those with experience in data flow diagramming seldom have the skills necessary to conduct structured interviews with harried users. It is much easier for systems analysts to assume user requirements from a limited data base (and then begin to specify a computer program) than it is to work closely with users over some period of time.

Perhaps even more amazing is the lack of emphasis placed on user requirements analysis in our colleges, universities, and professional schools. One would be hard pressed to find courses on user requirements analysis in any university; in fact, there are relatively few on software requirements analysis! Where do we suppose requirements analysis expertise comes from? It is unfathomable how the most important phase of any systems project is left to on-the-job trainers and trainees, and that we have failed to seriously attempt to elevate the requirements analysis process from a casual art to a rigorous science.

Users are inarticulate and inconsistent because it is inherently difficult to introspect upon one's own expertise. If I were to ask you to describe in the greatest of detail how you do what you do, would you find the challenge large or small? If I asked you to tell me precisely, completely, and unambiguously why you were good at what you do, could you do it? If I asked you to outline, prioritize, and interrelate your job functions, how hard would you find the assignment? How long would it take you to complete it? **Perhaps our expectations about user expertise are too high.**

Exacerbating the requirements analysis process is the lack of user technical expertise. Many users are computer "naive." They have had limited experience with anything but the most robust applications programs, like word processors and some database managers. They have probably experienced but a few input routines, and what little they often know about hardware borders on the dangerous. Systems analysts seldom disconnect from their lexicons long enough to establish real communication with users. Bits and bytes, RAM and ROMs, pull-downs, pop-ups, fields, and entities mean little to most users. There is, I suggest, a considerable amount of arrogance in many systems analysts. There is an attitude of "We are here to help you — aren't you lucky!" that defines many user/systems analyst relationships. Not surprisingly, users resent such attitudes and the behavior that they determine. If the truth be told, users should not care at all about the innards of the system intended to make them more productive; how many of us really understand how internal combustion engines work? Does it matter? Would it not be a waste of time to learn how everything works? Specialization calls for diverse and collaborative expertise. The good designer — the good systems analyst — adapts to the knowledge, experience, and needs of users; designers should never place the entire burden of communication upon the shoulders of those they are (allegedly) trying to help.

Maybe there are some "good" reasons why we don't like users very much; maybe there are some "good" reasons why they don't like us very much. Both hypotheses miss the point. We, as analysts and designers, have the primary responsibility to forge the necessary linkages with our users. We should fancy ourselves expert diagnosticians. We should perform like skilled and understanding physicians. We should expect users to behave like users. (As my four-year-old frequently reminds me when I complain about some strange, offensive behavior: "Well, Dad, kids are kids!") It is unrealistic for us to expect users to know about computing, to be forever available, consistent, and articulate, or to really care about our implementation problems. We must learn to understand and, yes, even like users. Until this state of mind is achieved, the gap between analysts and users will continue to widen, and if the gap gets any wider, our ability to design and develop useful, cost-effective systems may be permanently threatened.

WE DON'T APPRECIATE AVAILABLE METHODS

So how should we communicate with users? What methods, tools, and techniques are available? Are they any good?

Information systems design and development is multidisciplinary. It is absurd to think that computer scientists, electrical engineers, mathematicians, or cognitive psychologists can alone design, develop, or field good systems. If your experience has been discipline-based, then perhaps you now know why your systems haven't worked so well. When information systems were primarily embedded and when their contact with users was minimal, it was easier to build from a single perspective. This was especially true when systems were designed and developed by analysts and programmers who were also the users!

Things are very different today. Users are diverse in their skill and experience levels. Problems are more complex, often dynamic, and unyielding to anything but multidisciplinary solutions. Our underappreciation of available user requirements analysis methods suggests that we have not kept pace with the evolving world of problems we are supposed to conquer.

There are a variety of methods, tools, and techniques available to the modern user requirements analyst. They fall into two broad categories. The first category includes methods that by and large require us to ask users what it is that they do, how they do what they do, why they don't do what they do in some other ways, and the like. Without question, this is how most of us gather user requirements data. We often find it frustrating because it is such an imprecise process. It frequently yields precious little insight into what users need or want. The solution lies in the extent to which interaction with users is structured. There are thus structured and unstructured methods, tools, and techniques; the selection of one versus another always depends upon the characteristics of the users and the requirements problem, as well as the rate of analysis progress. In other words, if users are articulate and interested (which they are more likely to be if they are bona fide members of the systems design team), then it is sometimes possible to conduct unstructured, even ad hoc, interviews and gather a great deal of useful requirements data. If, on the other hand, the users are inarticulate and the problem area very complex, then interaction with users will have to be much more structured.

The second broad category of requirements analysis methods includes those tools and techniques that simulate or "game" requirements. Unlike methods, tools, and techniques based upon direct interaction with users, simulation and gaming techniques present users with opportunities to interact with problems and larger "scenarios." Some simulation methods do not even call for user participation, at least not in the same sense as participation takes place via an interview or requirements working group. Those divining requirements for the Strategic Defense Initiative (SDI), for example, must rely upon estimates and judgments about what the component SDI information systems must do, since there are very few users or analysts with space-based nuclear battle management experience.

H. Rudy Ramsey and Michael E. Atwood published a technical report more than a decade ago that identifies and assesses the various user requirements analysis methods. The figures that appear below are adapted from this report. Note the two basic "ask the user" approaches. One suggests that user requirements can be obtained via the use of questionnaires and surveys, and the other via interviews and field observation. What do you think of these alternatives? Clearly, interview and field observation are superior to questionnaire and survey-based methods. One could almost argue that the use of simple questionnaires — while inexpensive — is probably a waste of time. While there are certainly circumstances that might call for such methods, the kind of data one gets

Figure 1. Questionnaire and survey user requirements methods.

APPROACH	COMMENTS
Use of questionnaires to obtain ratings of the relative importance of various categories of information and system features.	Inexpensive. Difficult to be specific enough for detailed design decisions. Requires prior knowledge of all relevant information categories.
Use of questionnaires to obtain estimates of time spent on each task associated with recipient's job.	Self-estimates of time spent on work activities are notoriously poor. If only relative time is required, this may be adequate.
"Repertory Grid Technique," a questionnaire-based technique for determining users "cognitive frame of reference."	Difficult to use successfully. High-level, and may not easily be made specific enough for detailed design decisions.
"Delphi Technique," a survey technique in which recipient's responses are fed back anonymously. Recipient responds again, while aware of previous responses of entire group.	Relatively expensive. Promotes consensus and identification of all information categories, but may suppress important individual differences.
"Policy Capture," one of several techniques for developing quantitative relationships between perceived system desirability and specific system features.	Somewhat expensive. Mathematical assumptions may be inappropriate; paired-comparison procedure limits dimensionality.

from questionnaires is usually sparse and contradictory. This is especially true when the problem domain is very analytical.

Interview and field observation methods are more directly targeted at users and how they behave. What you can't get from an answer to a question, you can often get by watching the user performing the tasks earmarked for quasi- or full-automation. The mistakes we make here, however, are just as fatal as expecting too much from a questionnaire:

- We often rely too heavily on but one user.
- We often rely too heavily on different users at different phases of the analysis process.
- We don't do serious scheduling with users.
- We don't "manage" ad hoc working groups.
- We don't provide nearly enough feedback to users.
- We usually don't appoint requirements "czars" responsible for organizing the analysts and the users.
- We don't document the elicitation process and thereby fail to develop clear "audit trails" of our requirements analysis activities.
- We don't apply basic micro-project management principles to the process, principles that require the identification and tracking of milestones and deliverables (in this case, validated models of user requirements).

Figure 2. Interviews and field observation user requirements methods.

APPROACH	COMMENTS
Interviews with users to determine information requirements, decision points, organizational constraints, and the like.	Used more or less universally. Have many variants, such as "structured" interviews. Although a skilled interviewer can overcome some of the limitations of subjectivity and inability of users to verbalize their practice, these limitations are still significant. Most useful for preliminary data collection.
"Ad hoc working group," in which subject-matter experts devise system requirements by analysis and negotiation.	Appears somewhat effective at very high (undetailed) level. Has problems of subjectivity, and is susceptible to bias due to interpersonal relationships of group members (e.g., undue influence of high-status members).
"Critical Incident Technique,." in which users are asked, via interview or survey, for information about incidents of particular success or failure in the process of which the computer system will be a part.	A broadly useful technique which often yields significant insights into critical functions and information.
Job analysis techniques, such as task analysis, link analysis, and activity analysis, which attempt to characterize user behavior on the basis of direct observation.	Readily applicable to manual and clerical tasks, in which direct observation yields necessary raw data. Much more difficult to apply to cognitive tasks.

The problem we frequently encounter with simulation and gaming methods is that we often select poor scenarios from which to derive requirements. We also sometimes require users to become as familiar with the simulation (if users are directly involved) as they are expert in their respective problem-solving areas. Perhaps the best simulation-based method is protocol analysis, especially when coupled with a realistic scenario. Protocol analysis combines the best features of interview-, field observation- and scenario-based requirements analysis. The procedure is straightforward. All you need do is develop or select a good scenario and then ask users to solve the problems in the scenario — to simulate, if you will, how they would tackle the problems. In my own experience with tactical planning (user) requirements analysis, the technique has worked extremely well. In 1984, with the help of expert planners at the Army War College in Carlisle, Pennsylvania, I conducted a scenario-based protocol analysis that yielded solid insight into planning processes at the Army Corps level. The problem-solving sessions were videotaped so that we could subsequently and repeatedly study the planners at work. We have used the technique in several other instances with similar success. As always, however, it is necessary to have articulate, experienced users capable of "thinking aloud" as the scenario unfolds.

The methods in Figures 1, 2, and 3 — along with all of the hybrid possibilities — can be traced to a variety of fields of inquiry and formal disciplines. Requirements analysis methods owe their origins to

Figure 3. Simulation and gaming user requirements methods.

APPROACH	COMMENTS
"Paper" simulation in which the possible function of a computer system is simulated by human observers, in order to obtain information about the user's problem-solving and information-seeking behavior.	Relatively inexpensive, and often very informative. Can be used in very unstructured form, freeing user from dialogue constraints which might interfere with problem solving, or in very structured form to simulate exact properties of proposed system. Can be obtrusive, and requirement for manual computation can cause unacceptably slow simulation.
"Protocol," in which the user comments extensively on his activities during simulated problem solving, and formal content analysis of the resulting commentary ("protocol") is used to make inferences about user behavior and problem-solving processes.	Similar in many respects to paper simulation, but more obtrusive, more detailed. Transcription and scoring of protocols is very time-consuming, often restricted to a small number of cases. This is the indicated approach when a detailed problem-solving model is the goal.
Interactive simulation or gaming, in which the actual system, or an interactive computer simulation of the system, is used with a scenario to observe user behavior and system performance.	If done during initial design phase, this approach requires sophisticated software tools or expensive software development. It is very effective in identifying design defects and improving dialogue. Requires prior system design, and is, therefore, more appropriate for design evaluation iteration than for initial inquiry into user requirements.

the social, behavioral, computer, mathematical, engineering, and managerial sciences. Our search for additional methods should not be restricted to the fields or disciplines with which we feel the most comfortable. Strangely enough, the discipline that has contributed the most to user requirements analysis is psychology, not computer or systems science. The methods, tools, and techniques in the figures seldom appear in computer science curricula, nor are they generally taught in any of the engineering sciences. In order to design "hard" information systems, we must turn to the "soft" behavioral sciences.

We use the wrong methods at the wrong time. (They are usually in the wrong hands, anyway.) We underappreciate the utility of a variety of methods largely unknown to computer scientists, systems analysts, and engineers. We need to cast our requirements methodology nets much, much wider and exploit the capabilities of a large repertoire of tools and techniques with established track records.

WE GO TOO FAST

We expect far too much from single sessions with users. We unrealistically expect consensus among users after but a few interviews or hours with ad hoc working groups. We do not fully appreciate the imprecise nature of requirements analysis and the need to iterate on requirements data (with and without users) over some reasonable period of time. What is a "reasonable" period of time? The answer lies with the rate of progress made during the requirements analysis process. If consensus emerges among users early in the process, then requirements modeling (and verification) can proceed, but if consensus is difficult to forge, then more time and effort are clearly necessary. Project requirements often stimulate the unjustifiable acceleration of the requirements analysis process: managers want to see programmers at work as early as possible. They too often measure progress by counting lines of code, not by assessments about the quality of user requirements data.

We need to revise our estimates about how long it takes to identify, refine, and validate user requirements. We need to slow down, slow way, way down....

We also need to appreciate the importance of domain expertise. It is, according to many who have looked at the systems analysis process, difficult at best and usually quite impossible for analysts to do good requirements analyses without any understanding of the substance of the problem at hand (Curtis, et al., 1988). Good systems and requirements analysts study beforehand the "stuff" of what their users do and need done on the prospective system. If you send them out ignorant of the problem area, you send them out unprepared. Does this mean that systems analysts must become expert inventory controllers, tactical planners, and payroll specialists prior to designing systems that might help such folks? No. But it does mean that they must understand the basic concepts, tools, and — at a minimum — lexicon of the area.

WE SELDOM TAKE THE LONG VIEW

Requirements evolve over time. Users change after exposure to a new (or modified) system. Requirements analysis methods are only as good as the depth of their application. Capturing requirements data via one scenario or a single user is misleading at best, and threatens our ability to evolve a system's capabilities over time. Where will the system be in five years? Ten years? Who will the users be? What will they expect the system to be able to do with them, for them, and all by itself?

The long view should change the way we design. The long view requires flexibility. Designs that cannot breathe over time die expensive deaths. Because of the uncertainties in our procurement practices, "smart money" fixates on short-term payoff. Unfortunately, this makes for costly retrofitting. In order to preserve as many design options as possible, we must initially design for change. This, of course, is more expensive than static design and development, and therein lies the dilemma.

It is tempting to blame design myopia on the procurement process. Contractors frequently mumble to themselves about the unpredictability of support, the idiosyncratic nature of the "competitive" bidding process, and the contracting "life cycle" that jettisons contractors after but a few very successful years (when they're told that "a change is appropriate"). But another line of reasoning traces design inflexibility to our unwillingness to experiment with creative design principles, our inability to project future requirements, and our uncertainty about future technological capabilities.

The long view is essential to our long-term success. Given that we spend far more on software changes than we do on initial systems design and development, and given that the amount of money available for modifications will shrink over time, we had better begin to plan for the future now.

Whole new design strategies will be necessary. Future-oriented system designs must be developed to prevent prohibitively expensive retrofitting of inflexible systems. Without some major changes in the way we do business, we will remain shortsighted about the long view.

WE ALLOCATE TASKS POORLY

How do we decide who does what? How do we allocate tasks and power across the human and hardware/software components of modern systems? Does it make any sense to have overworked, highly stressed humans in air traffic control towers when computer-based systems could manage the skies much more efficiently? Is it prudent to allow human operators to override programmed responses to nuclear power plant emergencies? What about

Figure 4. Control trends and expectations.

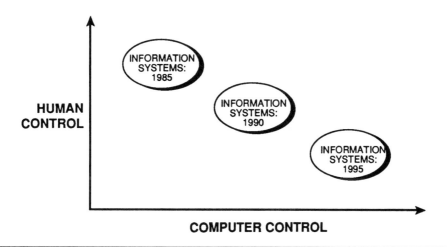

Figure 5. Allocation opportunities by analytical method.

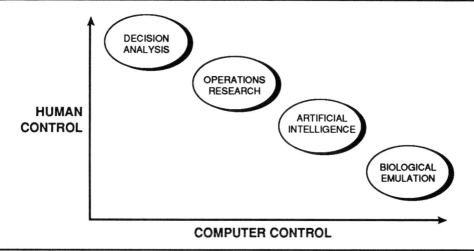

Figure 6. Allocation opportunities by method with "causal" pressures.

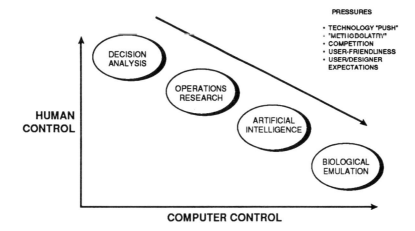

Figure 7. A prototyping life cycle.

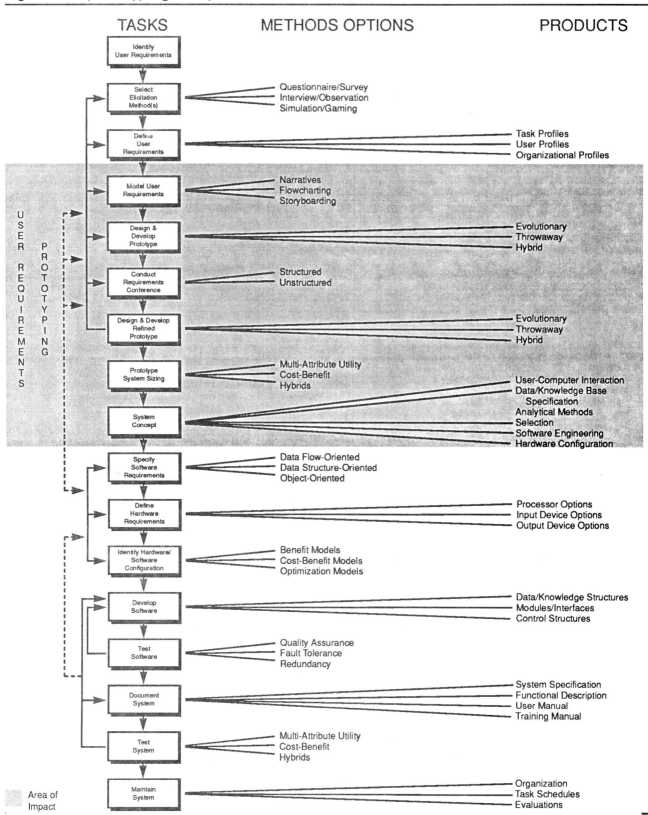

airplanes? If we could build an intelligent computer-based "pilot's associate," why should a human be in the cockpit? (Related to the question is Isaac Asimov's prediction about future cockpits. Asimov argues that there will be two organic beings in tomorrow's cockpits: one human and one canine. The dog will be there to keep the human from touching anything.)

Allocation is important because if we allocate tasks poorly, then we will not only spend far more than necessary to design and develop our systems, but may well undermine our most fundamental problem solving as well. There are countless examples of poor allocation strategies; there are systems under development today with ill-defined allocation strategies, systems — like those that will support the Strategic Defense Initiative (SDI) — that have important implications for our very survival.

The following figures suggest some relationships among computer control, human control, systems types, and some analytical methodologies. The figures suggest that it is now possible to allocate more decision-making power to our information systems, and that certain methods presume allocation strategies.

Requirements and our technological capabilities should determine how we allocate tasks, but this assumes that we have some procedures for optimally allocating tasks and, ultimately, power. Research in this area is absolutely critical to the design of cost-effective and reliable information systems. Suffice it to say here that many of our requirements and design failures can be traced to our inability to optimally allocate tasks between users and the systems with which they are expected to work, and that enormous leverage lies in the application of optimal allocation strategies.

WE UNDERAPPRECIATE THE POWER OF RAPID (AND NOT-SO-RAPID) PROTOTYPING

Prototyping is a euphemism for failure. It is amazing that the information systems community took so long to seize upon a concept that made iteration and bad initial design legitimate. (Incidentally, the appeal of this strategy has not escaped the artificial intelligence [AI] community.)

"Rapid prototyping" assumes that it is difficult if not impossible to capture user requirements early in the design process (Andriole, 1988, 1989; Boar, 1984; Gilhooley, 1987; Janson and Smith, 1985). Prototypers believe that "working models" of system concepts can facilitate communication among users and designers in some ways that words alone could never hope to facilitate. Prototyping provides a way to refine and validate user requirements. When done right, it is cost-effective. When done poorly, it can be expensive and sometimes even dangerous.

Nevertheless, we have yet to explore the real power of the approach. Over the past few years, we have engaged in prototyping at a variety of levels for a number of clients. Some of the prototypes were developed because user requirements were hard to refine and validate. Others were developed because we needed to "size" the system development effort before committing resources.

Figure 7 from Andriole (1989) suggests where prototyping occurs in the information systems life cycle. Figure 8 from Boar (1984) suggests the mini-life cycle that defines the prototyping strategy.

A few years ago, the famous Packard Commission (given the task to clean up defense and general government procurement and systems design processes) suggested that prototyping be made part of the standard design process. The recommendation was met with enthusiasm until incompatibilities between prototyping and mandated life cycle models (like those required by Department of Defense [DOD] Standards 2167A and 2168) were discovered. Prototyping is now force-fit into the "preliminary design" phases of traditional life-cycle models because — lip service aside — accepted life-cycle models simply do not recognize the premier role that prototyping should play in the systems design and development process.

Prototyping is the only sensible way to design and develop interactive systems intended to support analytical problem solving. The reasons are simple. First, analytical user requirements are inherently complex. Second, it is impossible to validate analytical user requirements without a working model of prospective system capabilities.

Figure 8. Boar's prototyping mini-life cycle.

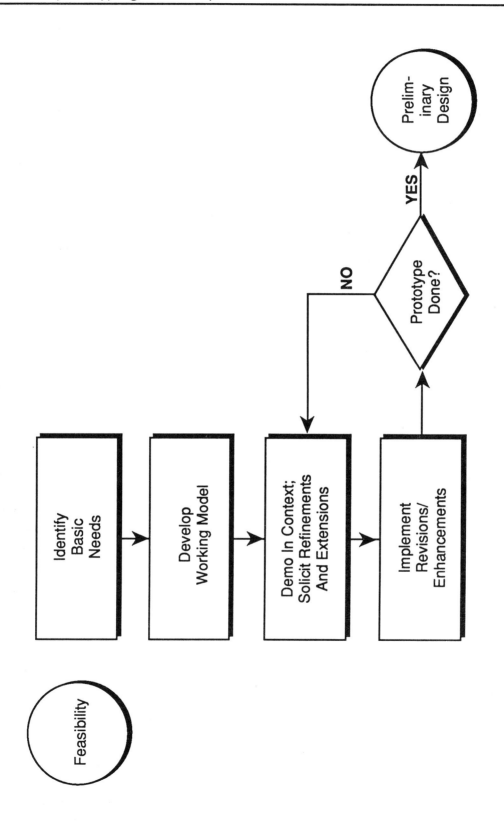

Figure 9. Task, user, and organizational requirements matrix.*

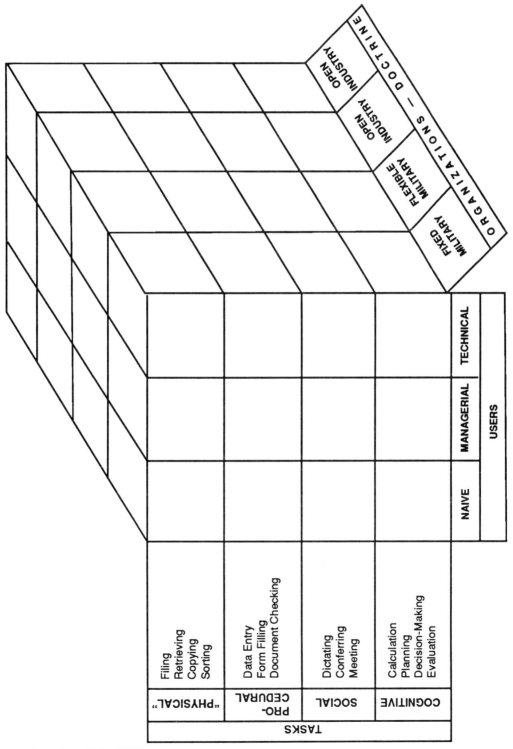

*Task categories are drawn from Galitz (1984).

Figure 10. The requirements/modeling/prototyping process.

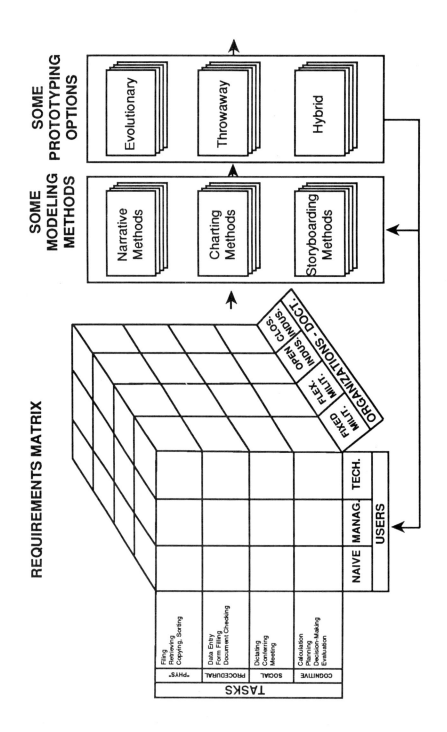

Figure 11. The iterative requirements analysis/prototyping process.

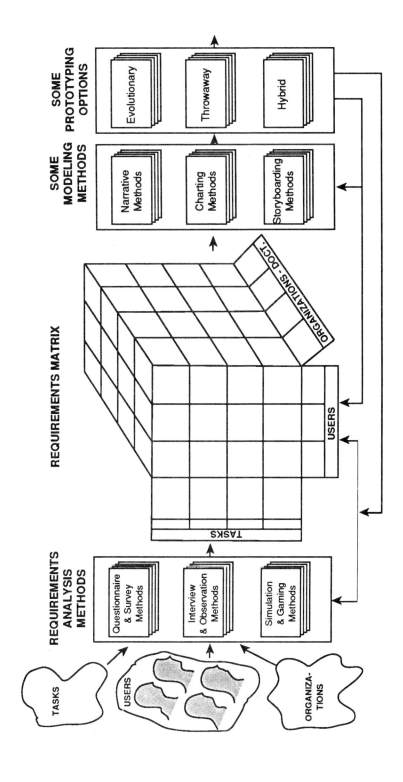

Third, it is impossible to "size" a prospective system — that is, determine its interface, software engineering, hardware, and knowledge-and/or database requirements — without a working prototype. There are derivative reasons, but the message is clear. Prototyping represents a sound "try-before-buy" strategy, a strategy that uncovers design flaws, costing issues and invalid requirements before expensive programming beings.

We have no prototyping database. We don't know how effective prototyping has been or how well it will serve a project at hand because we have failed to monitor how and under what circumstances it has been applied. Preliminary data (Andriole, 1988, 1989; Boar, 1984; Brooks, 1988; Gilhooley, 1987) suggests that the approach is extremely cost-effective. Such an early finding is intuitively obvious, but without hard data it is difficult to predict the value added via prototyping given a specific design problem. Nevertheless, from all indications, we have vastly underutilized the approach.

Unfortunately (and predictably), our expectations about what prototyping can do are too high. The very phrase, "rapid prototyping," suggests that the approach represents a design shortcut. This, of course, is a popular misconception, since prototyping — as Figures 7 and 8 illustrate — often requires iteration. Rapid prototyping thus sometimes evolves into not-so-rapid prototyping. While the latter form may take more time, the elongated process does not necessarily reflect the inappropriateness of the approach; quite to the contrary, successful prototyping prevents the release of a systems design until requirements have been validated via the working model. If it takes three or four (or five or six!) working models, then so be it; under no circumstances should system concepts be prematurely released.

WE DISREGARD CONTEXT

Systems never operate in a vacuum. One aspect of the requirements analysis process that is frequently ignored is the organizational/doctrinal context that will define precisely how a system is to serve a set of established operational policies and procedures. The requirements analysis process is not complete until we have validated data about the nature of the users, the tasks they will be performing on the prospective systems, and the organizational/doctrinal characteristics of the environment in which the system will operate.

Figure 9 suggests a requirement matrix that recognizes the importance of the interrelationships among user, task, and organizational/doctrinal requirements. The cells in the matrix represent design challenges. Prototyping should not proceed until the matrix is developed. As Figure 10 suggests, the requirements matrix informs the prototyping process; Figure 11 integrates the entire requirements analysis process, a process seldom implemented by systems analysts and programmers.

It is important to note once again that all of the topics covered in this article pertain to user requirements analysis problems and challenges. A properly "sized" prototype will lead to the specification of the computer program that will satisfy the requirements validated via the prototype(s). We know how to write software specifications. We don't always know how to identify, refine, and validate user requirements. Unfortunately, if user requirements are misunderstood, then software requirements will be meaningless. Substantial leverage can be gained by improving the user requirements analysis process. If we don't improve our relations with users, we will continue to develop and deploy systems that need constant (and expensive) attention.

ABOUT THE AUTHORS

Stephen J. Andriole *is George Mason Institute (GMI) Professor of Technology in the Department of Information Systems and Systems Engineering, School of Information Technology and Engineering, George Mason University (the State University in Northern Virginia). He is also the President and Chief Scientist of International Information Systems, Inc.*

Dr. Andriole was formerly the Director of the Defense Advanced Research Projects Agency's Cybernetics Technology Office, where he was also a Program Manager.

He is the author, editor, co-editor, and co-author of over twenty books, including Applications in Artificial Intelligence *(Petrocelli Books, Inc., 1986),* Principles of Command & Control *(AFCEA International Press, 1988), and* Storyboard Prototyping: A New Approach to User Requirements Analysis *(QED Information Sciences, Inc., 1989). He has recently published articles in* Large Scale Systems, *the* IEEE Transactions on Systems, Man & Cybernetics, *and* Defense Analysis. *He is a frequent contributor to edited volumes in information systems design, decision support systems technology, and analytical methodology.*

Dr. Andriole has designed and developed a number of interactive systems, including several planning, resource allocation, and information management systems. His most recent work resulted in a prototype group decision support system for planning and crisis management.

IMPLEMENTING AN INFORMATION ENGINEERING ENVIRONMENT AT NATIONAL LIBERTY CORPORATION

Peter Cola

Hundreds, if not thousands of information systems organizations are moving to a "CASE" or engineered software development environment. Lots are having difficulty, many will fail, many have failed. The story of change at National Liberty is heartening. Learning as they progressed, the IS staff successfully made the change from being one of the struggling many to become one of the productive few. The story is useful and instructive to all managers planning to move to a data-driven, automated, applications development environment.

INTRODUCTION

This paper describes how the IS organization at National Liberty Corporation successfully transformed itself from a process-oriented Cobol, Assembler, VSAM shop to an organization focused on architecture, information, CASE, and relational database. This was accomplished in one year, with no increase in staff and with *no* application systems failures.

One measure of success was our ability to deliver a major application system that was comprised of 32 DB2 tables with 6,173,552 rows, 45 on-line CICS screens, 450,000 lines of code, and a transaction rate of 10,000 per day. This was accomplished while establishing our new development platform that required us to restructure our organization, establish a new planning and development methodology, adopt the principles and tools for data modeling (PACDESIGN), establish a CASE environment (PACBASE), and establish a relational database management system (DB2).

THE NEED: DATA MODELS

During the first half of 1987, before the new technology was chosen, an IS team comprised of vice presidents, managers, technicians, and business analysts established a conceptual systems model. The model was aimed at streamlining the marketing work-flow process throughout the company, enhancing the creative capabilities for our advertising pieces, and improving the quality and controls of our marketing information. As the model was being refined and presented to our senior business unit executives, two high-level requirements became obvious:

- The marketing workflow process was data- and information-intensive and vulnerable to change.
- A system would require a high degree of flexibility to accommodate changes in markets, products, organization, and distribution channels.

It became clear to us that in order to establish a systems architecture, we needed to shift from a process-based design to a data design. We gave the challenge of establishing a data model to several members of the IS staff. After several frustrating weeks, we realized that we were lacking the experience, skills, and tools, "but not the desire," to get the job done.

At this point, it was clear to us that we had to change the way we traditionally developed systems even if we weren't yet clear on exactly what had to change. It was a little bit like being lost in a big city: "There were many directions in which we could go — all would lead somewhere, but only one would get us exactly where we wanted to go."

Concurrent with the establishment of the conceptual systems model, members of the IS staff were evaluating database management systems, fourth-generation languages, and CASE tools. The number of options available was overwhelming. What was becoming obvious to us was that a development platform should be as integrated as possible; encompass a methodology, modeling tools, and programmer productivity tools, and be tightly interfaced with a DBMS. We were starting to question whether or not such an integrated environment existed.

In order to speed our progress, we decided to seek consulting help to focus on the following objectives:

- help in the construction of our data models
- help selecting a DBMS that was matched to our application system and our environment
- help in determining the most appropriate development platform

The selection of a consulting firm was extremely important to us. We had carefully selected an IS team that was totally business oriented in their views and, as such, was very objective in reviewing our technology options. As a matter of fact, the team was not convinced that this was the most appropriate time to establish a new development environment. We needed to find a firm that believed that the business strategies and the application systems were of primary importance, that data modeling could, in fact, be done independent of the development environment and one that would help us in an objective evaluation of the tools needed (if any) to get the job done.

We interviewed numerous firms and found that they all were willing to pay lip service to the importance of the business environment, but were much more in tune with the purer technology issue and wanted to drive the process from an IS point of view. Then we found Performance Development Corporation. We immediately realized that we were talking to a company that was on the same wavelength with us, that felt comfortable in understanding our business first, that believed that business strategy drives technology strategy, and even understood the complex conceptual systems model that we had and could offer business-oriented design suggestions.

After we hired PDC, we realized an immediate benefit. Our project team that had been stalled in attempting to create our data models became instantly productive. It was now September 1987, and we set an aggressive target of year-end to complete the preliminary data models and the selection process for a DBMS and a development platform.

THE DILEMMA: A TECHNOLOGY PLATFORM

As we progressed with our data architecture, it became very obvious that the size and complexity of our system required a relational DBMS and that any of the best ones on the market would fit our requirements.

The selection of a development platform was a different matter. We focused on the culture of the company, management's expectations (both IS and corporate), the sophistication of the IS organization, and the amount of risk we were willing to take. To sum up our situation, we were a very aggressive marketing-oriented company; we believed in taking the shortest and least risky path; we typically expected immediate results; and our IS organization had a high degree of credibility and was more business oriented that technically oriented.

As we approached the end of the year, we had to decide between a fourth-generation language and CASE. The fourth-generation language was tightly coupled with a DBMS that offered immediate gains in programmer productivity; it was being successfully used in numerous organizations and was easy to learn and install. The integrated CASE environment cost twice as much, required a steep learning curve, and appeared to have more implementation failures than successes. The answer seemed obvious, but a few members of the team had become believers in CASE, and we could not reach a consensus.

As a result, I felt compelled to understand the trade-offs in benefits, the difficulties in attaining success, the magnitude of change required, and, most important, the management commitment that was going to be required in each situation.

THE VISION: THE ULTIMATE APPROACH TO PRODUCTIVITY

We had always taken a very pragmatic approach to systems development productivity. We focused on the number of hours being spent on maintenance, enhancements, small projects, and major projects, and consistently worked hard to shift as many of our resource hours to the work of highest value to the corporation.

At times, this required us to dramatically increase the effort on maintenance work in order to ultimately reduce the ongoing demand in this area. Over the years, we had reduced our maintenance workload from 40% to 11%.

We had a belief that project productivity was a complex management issue, so we focused on methodology, project management training, hiring the best people who understood our company's business, user involvement, high visibility, commitments to target get dates, mainframe response and turnaround time, rigid testing requirements, and a few meaningful productivity tools.

Reflecting on the whole issue of productivity, our past approaches, and the degree of success that we had in establishing a high level of credibility was very useful. It helped us to take a more holistic view of the benefits of CASE technology.

We began to develop a vision of a future systems development process that focused on the entire life cycle of a system and not just the life cycle of a project. We knew that the systems we needed to build were going to be evolutionary in nature and required a high degree of flexibility. We also realized that our systems architecture would continue to expand and incorporate many areas of the business and that reuseable code would provide the most dramatic benefit in the future.

We also saw a dramatic future benefit of establishing a discipline that integrated our specifications, data models, process models, documentation, screens, code, data elements, and data dictionaries. The repository concept took on a whole new meaning for us as being the central controlling entity around which all of our standards and disciplines would revolve.

As we thought about populating the repository with "reuseable everything," our imaginations ran wild with opportunities of engineering valuable time out of our future development efforts. Suddenly, the opportunities for prototyping, screen painting, and code generation were merely icing on the cake. The obvious choice suddenly shifted. The questions now were: "Are we up to the challenge? Will senior management and our user community be patient enough to allow us to totally change our development environment? Will our highly skilled staff accept the obvious change in methodology and behavior that would be necessary to make this work?"

THE COMMITMENT: TIME, MONEY, TRUST, PATIENCE

The vision helped us to understand the opportunity for future benefits and the complexities involved in being a total success. We knew we would need to restructure our organization and shift some of our best systems development people into data administration and CASE administration. We realized that we needed to abandon our current methodology and adopt a new one; we needed to rewrite our standards; we needed to install and learn DB2; we needed to learn data modeling techniques and tools; we needed to master a very structured specification language; and the list went on.

Was our staff up to this challenge? We believed they were. They were hardworking, dedicated, business oriented, results oriented, stable, and ready to take on the challenge of building our future systems. They were so ready that they began to abandon their biases on which approach to take. In short, they were the strongest group of people that I had been associated with in 20 years.

We decided that the vision and challenge would be theirs, and we would not go out and hire experienced people. Instead, we would invest in consulting and training support to help us through the implementation, an implementation that we believed would take a year.

Would our company's senior management be willing to wait a year to receive their first systems deliverable? Would they be willing to give $1.5 million for software, training, and consulting fees? We believed they would. We felt that we had established enough credibility and a good enough partnership with them that they would take the time to understand our vision, trust our judgment, and have the same degree of confidence in us that we had. Perhaps the real question was whether or not we were willing to put this belief to the ultimate test.

There was another nagging issue to face: if we got the commitment, would we be able to keep it? We did have a history of impatience and expecting quick results. We had established a concept of having executive briefings on major projects in which we would discuss progress, expectations, issues, and changes in direction or benefits. We decided that we would use this forum to keep our senior executives involved every month and, therefore, retain their support.

We also had one other very important factor in our favor: a CEO who believed in the strategic importance of the systems we needed to build and, more important, who had the knowledge and experience to appreciate our challenge and commitment.

THE NEXT STEPS: LEARN TO SWIM BY JUMPING IN

Our belief in this vision and our level of conviction was high. On January 7, 1988, we presented our plan and gained approval to acquire and implement PACBASE and DB2.

The very next day we shared the decision and vision with the entire management staff. The managers became disciples and helped build the courage and enthusiasm for their people to tackle the task at hand.

We began our implementation planning immediately. We relied on the consulting services of Performance Development Corporation and CGI (our CASE vendor) to help us pave the way.

We selected 18 people (33%) out of our Systems Development group to form our pilot project team. Ultimately, these individuals were going to work in Data Administration, CASE Administration, or Systems Development. For now, their jobs were to learn all aspects of utilizing our new development platform and determine the best method of integrating the methodology, CASE, and DBMS together and into our environment. They would spend seven months on a relatively small project, but when they were finished, we would understand how and when to move developers into the new stages of development; how to control a project; how to balance the staffing levels between the development teams and data administration; the required training and learning and learning curve needed when moving new people into a CASE project; and so on.

We also ended up with a new methodology for planning, architecture, development, and maintenance. We established policies, procedures, standards, and departmental interfaces. We literally revolutionized our entire approach toward development.

The learning curve was definitely steep and, at times, the frustrations were high. We encountered obstacles with software problems, integration problems, and methodology confusion. Our group of 18 never stopped driving for perfection. Their dedication was a major key to success.

The commitment from the remaining areas of our IS organization was high as well. The remaining systems developers were carrying an increased workload in order to keep as much of our normal project workload progressing. Technical Services had to install and integrate the new software products into our environment and begin to monitor the performance impact of CASE and DB2. Our Security and Contingency Services area had to deal with the new environment. Our "users" (we refer to them as partners) had to get accustomed to a new vocabulary and new approach from us.

As we felt comfortable in having mastered or

established a stage in the life cycle of our pilot project, we began to educate more of our systems engineers in that stage so they could actually begin another project. As a result, we ended the year with 25 trained developers who were effectively working on four major projects.

In 1989, we are picking up a tremendous head of steam on our new development efforts. By the end of the year, we should have trained 85% of our developers on the new platform and provided all of them with the opportunity to work with the new methodology. Everyone is sensing a high degree of success in their ability to effectively meet our business needs. The number of disciples has multiplied, and they are focused on creating the ultimate development environment.

SUMMARY: ISSUES TO CONTEMPLATE

The following bullet points should provide food for thought in evaluating the potential for success in establishing an Information Engineering environment within your company:

- **People** — Do you have the staff that it takes to make it happen? Are they prepared for a new psychological contract?
- **Alignment** — of business plan and systems plan: Is there common ground on which to gain the commitments needed?
- **Vision** — Is the organization aligned and committed to the ultimate goal?
- **Credibility** — Does the IS organization have the backing that it needs to gain the support for a long-term commitment?
- **Commitment** — Do you understand the total commitment that is required within the company? Can you gain and sustain the commitment? Manage the expectations?
- **Consultants** — Do you know when you need them and how to use them? Does their style and approach match yours, and will they help your staff attain a higher level of knowledge and experience?

ABOUT THE AUTHOR

Peter A. Cola *is Vice President of Information Services and Marketing Operations for National Liberty Corporation, Valley Forge, Pennsylvania, an affiliate of Capital Holding Corporation.*

Mr. Cola is also responsible for the Information Systems Division of Capital Holding's Worldwide Insurance Group, located in St. Louis, Missouri. The combined operations of National Liberty and Worldwide form the Direct Response Group for Capital Holding.

Mr. Cola joined National Liberty in June of 1984. Previously he had been with J.C. Penney Life Insurance Company and Great American Reserve in Dallas, Texas, for seven years, with responsibilities for their information systems. Prior to 1977, Mr. Cola held positions with Anderson Clayton Corporation and IBM.

IT'S TIME FOR MIS TO CHANGE THE IMAGE OF FAX

Ralph D. Loftin

The advertisements claim that facsimile transmission has been around nearly as long as the automobile. At least three companies claim to have invented the technique of moving a facsimile of a document over telephone or radio transmission.

Like many of us, facsimile transmission (which we've nicknamed "fax") was a slow bloomer. As it approaches its 60th birthday, it is finally getting some respect and a lot of use.

Many in the traditional MIS organization have not treated fax with enough respect. If the discussion is termed "image processing," heads nod knowingly. Integrating the fax phenomenon into the fabric of the information architecture of the firm is a "must do" task with significant productivity and market opportunity.

INTRODUCTION

The facsimile (fax) machine has become as ubiquitous as the telephone in the business office. A recent poll by First Copy indicated that after the telephone, word processor, and copier, the fax machine was considered to be the most important piece of office equipment.

The exchange of printed documents is now as easy and instantaneous as the exchange of voice messages or computer files. A new dimension has been added to business communications, offering new opportunities for businesses to improve service and responsiveness. Delicatessens receive carryout orders by fax; restaurants take reservations by fax; lawyers exchange contracts with clients by fax; corporations handle special service requests via fax. The question is no longer, "Do you have a fax machine?" but rather, "What is your fax number?"

With only 15% of the market penetrated (*Fortune*, June 19, 1989), fax machine sales are expected to grow at a compounded annual rate of more than 60% through 1994, at which time the installed base of fax machines will reach nearly 8 million units. By 1991, worldwide fax traffic is expected to approach 60 *billion* pages!

However, the explosive growth in fax traffic has created frustrating, inefficient, and costly bottlenecks in the use of individual fax machines. Most faxs are not integrated into a firm's management information network, and the use of fax machines remains, in many ways, unmanaged.

THE TROUBLE WITH FAX

For all their value, fax machines present a number of unresolved operational problems. As fax traffic grows, these problems grow more severe — and in most companies the extent and cost of these problems are completely unknown except to those who are victimized by them.

Problem 1 — Faxs Are Labor-Intensive

Most large companies have installed several forms of office automation, and have enjoyed a resulting increase in office productivity. In some firms, one secretary will support more than a dozen professionals or executives.

However, sending a document with a fax machine requires that the document first be printed, then carried to the fax machine. The receiver's fax number must then be dialed — usually a manual operation often involving busy lines and retries. Finally the document must be hand-fed through an electromechanical device and the transmission monitored to assure that the document was received successfully. Often there are voice telephone calls to confirm that the document actually arrived and was legible.

Similarly, a document received at a fax machine must be hand-delivered to the recipient and copied and distributed to others as needed.

Problem 2 — Fax Machines Can Compromise Security

Sensitive and urgent information is frequently sent by fax. Yet, because of the nature of faxs sent through machines, it is not unusual for several people to see a faxed message before it reaches its intended recipient.

Problem 3 — The Use of Fax Machines Is Costly

Fax machines and associated telephone costs represent an ever-increasing expense which is difficult to control. The cost of fax machines and additional phone lines required for fax operation add up quickly. In addition, most faxs are sent during business hours, thus incurring peak telephone charges.

Problem 4 — Access To Fax Machines Is Uncontrolled

Once installed, fax is used often — sometimes frivolously and sometimes without authorization. This unrestricted ability to send documents anywhere, immediately, on company letterhead contributes to additional security problems, not to mention increased costs.

Problem 5 — Faxed Messages Stall En Route

Faxed messages can cross a continent at the speed of light, but in order for a fax message to reach its destination, it often goes through *two* company mail rooms or centralized fax machines. At either end, it must either be delivered or picked up by messenger. For urgent messages, this is an unacceptable and, again, unsecure delivery method.

Problem 6 — Fax Machines Are Breakable

The fax machine, with its moving parts, is another piece of office hardware that can and does break down. Jammed paper, spilled coffee, and other mishaps do occur, and always at inopportune times.

Problem 7 — Poor Quality of Fax Documents

The majority of fax machines produce documents on specially coated paper. The images on this paper are often indistinct, and will fade after several months. In addition, the paper tends to curl; is less durable, and is vulnerable to tearing, marking, and discoloration. Some machines produce documents on one continuous strip, requiring multiple pages to be separated manually, usually in irregular lengths.

BRINGING FAX INTO THE MIS INFRASTRUCTURE: REQUIREMENTS FOR SOLUTIONS

The answer to these problems is not to add more fax machines, but that is exactly what most organizations are pressured to do. The real solution is to incorporate fax technology into the MIS infrastructure so that fax messages can be managed cost-effectively. Fax should be approached by the MIS manager as one more office automation opportunity.

To accomplish this requires that the MIS manager demonstrate to the corporation the advantages of an integrated approach. Happily, new products are becoming available which make these advantages abundantly clear. However, before examining these options in detail, consider what features and capabilities the ideal solution to the fax problem should offer.

The Corporate Fax Environment

Integrating fax into the MIS technology platform recognizes that the vast majority of documents which are sent by fax are generated on computers, and particularly personal computers. In addition, personal computers in most corporations are networked, primarily with LANs.

Thus the requirements outlined below are described for a corporate environment where personal computers are assumed to be connected to others via a local area network (LAN), and connected via a LAN gateway to public or private networks, to a mainframe, or to other LANs.

The user is taken to be someone who uses a personal computer in this networked environment to create a document which might include text, graphics, spreadsheets, and database outputs. In addition, it is assumed that this document might need to be combined with photographs or other original documents, and faxed to any fax machine worldwide. It is also assumed that this user will receive faxes from multiple sources outside the corporation. Finally, it is assumed that the user will want to share faxes, both sent and received, with others in the corporation.

Labor-Saving Features

Sending a fax using a fax machine requires that the sender print a document, hand-carry that document to the fax machine, phone the receiver, and feed the document into an electromechanical device. The user should be spared all of these steps, and in addition should be able to automatically create a fax transmittal sheet.

The user should automatically be able to send multiple documents to the same destination in a single transmission.

Delivery of faxed messages should be practically guaranteed. Pages which are not successfully transmitted due to telephone line problems should be automatically retransmitted until they are successfully received, or discontinued by the sender.

The same fax message should be easily broadcast to multiple locations.

Money-Saving Features

When only the content is important, the user should be able to send faxes in "draft quality" to save transmission time and cost.

The user should be able to schedule faxes automatically to be sent during times when phone rates are lower.

Multiple telephone trunks should be available to reduce contention for telephone lines and to reduce the costs of long-line vendor routing of fax messages.

A log of all faxs sent and received should be maintained so that the true cost of fax can be monitored and allocated appropriately. Expenses can then be billed according to departmental use rather than being treated as a general and administrative expense. Unnecessary faxes can be eliminated, and the overall cost of fax services can be reduced substantially.

Features That Reduce Copying and Distribution

Letterhead images should be easily captured and stored, allowing computer-generated documents to be electronically placed on company letterhead.

Compound documents should be easily created by merging the output of word processors with that of graphics and spreadsheet packages, and even images created by scanners (including fax machines). These compound documents can then be faxed as an integrated message or sent across the network to another workstation using the existing E-mail system.

Incoming fax messages should be received directly at the user workstation, providing instant, secure delivery.

Fax transmissions, both sent and received, should be easily forwarded to one or more other users connected to the LAN.

Faxs should be easily viewed on the PC monitor instead of being printed, thus saving both time and paper.

The user should have the option to store incoming fax messages on a local disk or diskette for later viewing, printing, or archiving.

Security Features

The ability to save time by sending fax messages from every desk must be counterbalanced by the ability to control access to the resource. Several levels of control should be provided. Users should be provided with valid ID/password combinations to utilize the fax server. Additionally, all fax traffic should be logged for audit purposes.

Additional security levels should be provided through a dial-back feature which automatically hangs up on the caller and dials the sender's known number to insure that erroneous messages are not coming from unauthorized sources. This feature will also effectively screen junk faxes.

The user signature should be easily scanned and placed in a secure file. The signature should then be able to be placed in any position on documents when they are ready to be faxed.

All inbound and outbound fax messages should be logged to a disk file. This file provides an audit trail detailing fax use by user ID and department, including number of pages sent and received, time of activity, the remote user ID, and any error codes.

Convenience Features

The user should select action items from menus, thus reducing the possibility of keying errors.

Frequently called numbers should be maintained in an electronic phone book for quick reference and fax addressing.

Fax numbers should be dialed automatically from a phone number database, thereby minimizing costs associated with misdialed numbers.

The user should have the option to send urgent fax messages immediately. Classes of service should be definable for various types of users.

The user should be able to create and send a fax from within any application, without leaving the application. Word processing, spreadsheet, or graphics files should be converted automatically to fax format and sent without the need for printing.

The user should not be required to execute any operating system instructions to create and send a fax. All instructions and commands should be intuitively obvious.

A file system should be provided to allow the user to store fax messages, both sent and received. This file system should allow for personal files, shared files on the LAN server, and corporate files which can be accessed from any workstation on any LAN.

Creating, sending, and receiving faxes should not interfere with any aspect of the existing technical environment, including LAN software and electronic mail systems. Similarly, the user should not be required to utilize special E-mail software in order to send, receive, or share faxs.

Documents should be accepted from document scanners, including fax machines, and incorporated with others for subsequent fax transmission.

Spreadsheets and other documents which are received in landscape mode should be easily rotated for horizontal viewing.

Inevitably some fax pages will be received upside down, according to the way they are placed in the machine when sent. These pages should be easily inverted for viewing.

The fax image should be able to be viewed easily and naturally in order to avoid printing. Small images or dense areas should be able to be magnified when necessary for clarity. The user should be able to pan and scroll smoothly around the image.

THE OPTIONS FOR SOLUTIONS

MIS managers who seek to provide an integrated fax capability for their corporations have three product options available:

1. mainframe-attached network servers
2. individual PC fax boards
3. LAN network servers

Mainframe-attached fax servers are vastly more expensive than the other options, both in terms of purchase price and support required. These devices allow faxs to be sent without the need to print the document, but typically do not permit the users to view received faxs. All received faxs are printed and routed manually. While well suited to some particular high-volume applications, these devices do not match well with the general requirement for most corporations.

PC-fax boards are distinguished by the software which allows the PC user to manipulate fax images before and after transmission. Most PC-fax boards are similar in their technical capabilities, except for slight differences in compatibility with printers and scanners. They are limited to use by a single PC, will not operate on LANs, are not directly programmable, and require relatively sophisticated and complex user intervention. In addition, each PC requires a dedicated telephone line, defeating some of the cost savings potential of MIS/fax integration. Although useful, these products remain clumsy and complex for all but the relatively sophisticated PC user.

The best of the LAN-based fax servers allow networked PCs to exchange fax messages with fax machines, but also allow fax documents to be sent as messages through the corporate E-mail system. Combined with a powerful yet simple user interface, these products allow users to assemble documents which combine text, graphics, spreadsheets, and images, and send these documents as integrated messages, either to fax machines or to other corporate users.

These devices also permit the sharing of telephone lines, thus leading to substantial savings over individual fax machines and PC boards. All the users on a LAN can have a fax capability for the price of two or three individual PC-fax boards. In short, these products offer the best match for the requirements shown above, and are recommended as the first approach for the MIS manager.

Combining the money saving features of such a device with its productivity enhancements, adopting a LAN-based fax server approach can be easily cost-justified.

- **Labor Requirements Are Reduced.**
  The need for added labor is eliminated because faxs can be sent and received at the desk of the sender or receiver. If the recipient is busy elsewhere, the message can be routed to where he or she is, or stored in the recipient's computer for later viewing.
- **Delivery Of Sensitive Information Is Secured.**
  Incoming fax messages are automatically routed through the PC-LAN directly to the PC on the recipient's desk. Neither incoming nor outgoing messages are required to be handled by intermediaries. (See Appendix A for a brief description of some of the methods available for routing incoming fax messages.)
- **Telephone Charges Are Decreased.**
  A sending queue is maintained that is sensitive to message priority, requested time to send the message, and requested communications path. Faxs are sent in less time, over optimal routes, and during off-peak hours when requested.
- **Access To Fax Is Controlled.**
  An activity and message log is maintained containing data on user activity, call duration, and peak and lull activity periods. In addition, automatic dial-back security ensures a sender's validity.

The best of the LAN-based fax servers can reduce operational costs by employing various technologies that: (1) reduce the length of each transmission; (2) schedule transmissions for off-peak rates; and (3) reduce the labor needed to prepare a document for transmitting through fax. In addition, the labor component of fax cost is dramatically reduced because paper and the associated handling costs are eliminated.

This combination of features provides management control of fax transmissions, increases the utility and power of installed PCs and PC-LANs and saves users money while smoothing work flows. These are the underlying reasons for office automation, and they apply emphatically where fax technology is concerned.

The MIS manager has the opportunity to bring a valuable service to the corporation, and to demonstrate hard dollar savings in the process. The image of fax can and should be changed by MIS. Perhaps in the process the image of MIS will also be enhanced.

APPENDIX: A NOTE ABOUT ROUTING RECEIVED FAXS

For users who share a common send/receive device (a fax server), there are four ways to accomplish routing of received faxes to the proper workstation. At the most rudimentary level, all inbound faxes can be held at a server, and an individual designated to review and forward them to the appropriate workstation. This approach has the advantage of simplicity, but requires frequent intervention by an individual. This intervention can compromise security for sensitive documents, and can introduce delays.

A step up in sophistication and automation utilizes an approach called Digital Tone Multiple Frequency (DTMF). Each workstation sharing the server is assigned a unique three- or four-digit number as an address. The sender of the fax must dial the fax telephone number and wait for the server to answer. Upon hearing the response tones, the sender then enters the number corresponding to the unique workstation address of the recipient. Software in the fax server then interprets the number and routes the fax to the appropriate workstation automatically.

The advantage of the DTMF approach is that no human intervention is required at the receiving end, but the disadvantage is that the sender is required to monitor the fax transmission and key in additional numbers.

Another step up in sophistication utilizes Direct Inward Dialing (DID), which is available in most areas from the local telephone company. In this method, the user must purchase a DID trunk, a group of 100 contiguous telephone numbers, from the local telephone company. Each workstation sharing the server is assigned a unique telephone number from the group. The sender need only dial the unique telephone number. All the numbers in the DID group ring through the single DID trunk at the fax server. The server then "winks" back to the telephone company central office to request the exact number which was called. Upon receiving the exact number from the central office, the server then receives the fax and routes it to the appropriate workstation. The obvious advantage to this approach is that each workstation on the LAN can have a unique fax telephone number. A disadvantage is that the cost of the DID trunk may be prohibitive for some organizations. In addition, DID trunks can only receive faxes; separate telephone lines are required for sending. Also, fax server products which offer this feature may be substantially more costly.

The final routing method involves the use of pattern recognition technology. In this method, the fax sender includes a routing page which contains a symbol corresponding to the network address of the recipient. Software in the server translates the symbol and routes the incoming fax accordingly. The advantage of this approach is that the sender may send faxes to multiple recipients on the LAN with a single telephone call by including a separate routing page for each. The disadvantage is that the sender must create a directory of fax addresses which includes symbols as well as telephone numbers.

ABOUT THE AUTHOR

Ralph D. Loftin *has worked more than 20 years in a variety of management positions with increasing responsibility in the areas of information systems and services . . . particular skills in strategic and tactical planning, organizational effectiveness, vendor relationships and contract management, operations performance, and capacity and resource management.*

As Vice President of Data Processing Services for Blue Cross and Blue Shield of Massachusetts, a $4 billion health care services company, Ralph Loftin had complete Information Resource Management responsibility, including voice and data communications, reprographics and micrographics, mail operations, word processing, and data processing. He managed a staff of 700 and an annual budget of $35 million.

Previously, at General Electric's Information Services Division, he developed a programming service business for both government and commerical markets. He was responsible for marketing and sales, contract administration, and project management and control.

For the same firm, Ralph also managed a contractor support group for a major NASA installation, furnishing programming, hardware engineering, and equipment maintenance services.

He holds M.S. and B.S. degrees in Electrical Engineering from the Georgia Institute of Technology. Author of numerous papers and articles, he has spoken widely at national and international conferences. His work in the use of organizational effectiveness methods in managing the information systems function was the subject of a prize-winning paper in the 1982 Society for Information Management national competition.

Ralph Loftin serves on the National Executive Council for the Society of Information Management and was Chairperson of the Boston Chapter. He has taught at Georgia Tech, the University of Massachusetts, and Babson College and is on the adjunct faculty at Suffolk University. He was appointed to the National Panel of Arbitrators in 1973.